TEACH

Lessons I Learned from My Students and Colleagues

MICHAEL UNGER

Cover image by Vondrell Swain, class of 2011

Printed in the United States of America
Published by Braughler Books LLC., Springboro, Ohio

First printing: 2022

ISBN: 978-1-955791-46-5 soft cover
ISBN: 978-1-955791-47-2 ebook

Library of Congress Control Number: 2022918058

Ordering information: Special discounts are available on quantity purchases by bookstores, corporations, associations, and others. For details, contact the publisher at:

sales@braughlerbooks.com

or at 937-58-BOOKS

For questions or comments about this book, please write to:

info@braughlerbooks.com

Braughler™
Books
braughlerbooks.com

For Yolanda and Bridget

Dedication

Mostly, I dedicate this book to Yolanda, a "loving gift."
She is a constant source of inspiration,
selflessness and courage.
Her struggle with cancer has shown me
how to live and how to die.

To my daughter, Emily who loves life in Chicago.

To my brother, Dan, and his wife Jane,
who have supported my many battles.

To my brother John, a Vietnam Veteran, and his
wife Marsha for always being so inspirational.

I would also like to dedicate this book to the
thousands of resilient urban public school students,
who inspire me every day, and to those special
colleagues who love the challenge to
TEACH.

"I will try to make myself available to my pupils. I believe neither that they will succeed nor that they will fail. I know they will fight, falter, and rise again and again, and that if I have the strength I will be there to rejoice and cry with them."

Herbert Kohl

Contents

Foreword

"Alright folks, get out your current events!" Each day he walked into class you were given the most current information that was available locally, in the state, the country and the world! To us city children, this was groundbreaking. The level of exposure that we had in this class blew our understanding of the world wide open and left most of us yearning to know as much as we could.

There is a certain duty that comes with being an Urban Educator and this particular teacher embodies all the qualities that have inspired hundreds of students over the course of 50 years in the classroom. No stranger to answering the call of responsibility as a veteran, I would be willing to bet that he gave his all to not only serving his country but his classroom as well.

I share with you a story that begins full of questions and mystery that now had led to me writing the forward of one of my greatest inspirations in the world.

As a young curious student who had just received his Freshman schedule I saw the name "Unger" and wasn't sure who it was. Before my mother pulled away from the school's parking lot, I saw a man walking to his car and my first thought was to ask him to identify himself so I knew who my American History teacher was going to be. So I rolled down my window and shouted "Excuse me sir!" The man turned around and replied "Yes?" All I wanted was a simple answer so I asked a simple question, "Are you Mr. Unger?'. As I waited in suspense, he looked and smirked, just a tad, and said "You'll find out." He proceeded to walk to his car and I thought, "if that is Mr. Unger, I'm scared!" School started and sure enough, the man I asked to identify himself turned out to be my American History teacher and my life would change forever.

I must say that while the anticipation was high to know the man behind the name, the experience and education that we all received was worth it. Mr. Unger has helped so many students see the light in themselves when we could see no such thing. He gave us the space to be ourselves and have real world conversations in class which were both therapeutic and deeply educational. Most importantly, he saw us for us. Public school kids, such as myself, have a wide range of circumstances that can surface at any given time. While not knowing exactly what we're going through, Mr. Unger knew and still knows that listening to us, being there for us, and believing in us can heal a lot of the wounds that we bear.

Mr. Unger has inspired so many of us students who struggled to find inspiration in ourselves. I teach because I was taught well and believe in carrying the torch. It is a true honor to wish you "happy reading" as you get a glimpse of the work he is capable of doing.

I hope this book finds all of you inspired and ready to help the children in your current or future classrooms the way Mr. Unger's class prepared me for my own to continue on with the necessary work for our future.

Unger, you're the GOAT.

Love,
Ivory L. Kennedy Jr.

STUDENT PROFILES

Do You See Yourself In The Kids?

As a storyteller, I often think about communication. How do we think, speak, and act? I want the whole story. I want to understand the characters, seeking to reveal their compassion, resilience, and determination. To understand, I think, means to be vulnerable. There is a wild vulnerability in being real and speaking the truth regardless of our anxieties. It's an honor to have the platform to open our hearts and minds and tell the complex narratives of ordinary people doing extraordinary things. The stories need to be told because they are a call to understand and to take action for our urban students.

Each student brings something unique to our classrooms in a "Figurative Bag." Several years ago I was asked by my principal to explain to the entire teaching staff how I look at the young people who walk into my room each day. I began by saying, "There are students that are similar to us, and there are students that are dissimilar." They can bring so many different life experiences in their "bag" such as:

- Coming from a one parent household.
- Living in a two-parent household.
- Having or not having health insurance.
- Going to pre-school.
- Experiencing death in the immediate family,
- Being a primary caretaker.
- Dealing with some form of sexual abuse.
- Living with different levels of depression or anxiety.
- Living with a disability.

- Surviving cancer or some other crippling disease.
- Having been bullied or being a bully.
- Participating on a competitive sports team.
- Having a special artistic talent.
- Living with large amounts of anger, built up over time.
- Having siblings or being an only child.
- Having a travel experience with parents.
- Being read to and liking to read.
- Experiencing love, having partial love, or having no love at all.

These students, with their individual bags, are the fabric of who we TEACH. Their stories demand to be heard. Our responsibility is to recognize and plant a seed of hope and opportunity no matter what positive or negative characteristics they "carry in their bag." Do you see yourself in the kids? They are valued because you see them, hear them, and understand them.

Every Person Has Challenges

Jacob • Shantel • George • Karah

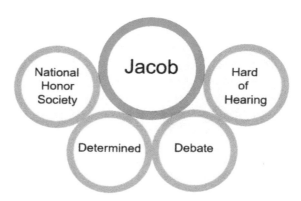

Jacob was introduced to me on the first day of class in early August by his American Sign Language (ASL) interpreter, Diana Gunckel. I didn't know what to expect because in my nearly 45 years of teaching, I've never had a student who was profoundly deaf.

Jacob lives with Usher's Syndrome. He was deaf "in utero" and he can't see in the dark. Usher's Syndrome is a condition characterized by partial or total hearing loss or vision loss that worsens over time. The hearing loss is classified as sensorineural, which means it is caused by abnormalities in the inner ear. The vision loss is caused by an eye disease called retinitis pigmentosa. Researchers have identified three major types of Usher's Syndrome, designated as types 1, 2, and 3, with their own subtypes as well. Jacob was diagnosed somewhere between Type 1 and Type 2. Usher's Syndrome accounts for ten percent of all cases of moderate to profound deafness in children. Presently, there's no cure for Usher's Syndrome, so we can only manage hearing, vision, and balance. Fortunately, the ASL Institute has contributed to helping people who are profoundly deaf.

Jacob

I placed Jacob's seat in the very front row of the room, with Diana facing him. The rest of the class could see Diana work her magic. Much of the time, I could see my students focus not only on me, but also on Diana's hands. They were in awe of how fast she could interpret my words for Jacob since I speak quickly anyway.

Jacob was very gifted academically. He was in the National Honor Society and always maintained an A average. He was inquisitive, and he constantly wanted clarification in my lectures. Diana was always well prepared for every lesson. She always knew ahead of time what vocabulary and objectives I was going to use. How do you interpret such concepts as federalism and *McCulloch vs. Maryland?* How do you convey what a filibuster is in terms of how a bill is passed? What is judicial review as validated by *Marbury vs. Madison?* What is gerrymandering? How does that fit? Bottom line is, Diana did her homework, and she always interpreted so Jacob knew the material.

She could sign the terms and spell them multiple times, and she usually had to do that because Jacob worked so hard with his spelling, grammar, and comprehension. Periodically in class, we would conduct debates according to the Ohio Speech and Debate rules. Jacob asked once if he could participate in a debate, and my answer was that absolutely he could.

He took the pro side in an argument about the legalization of marijuana for recreational and medicinal use. He and Diana did a superb job. Jacob was able to cite enough sources and evidence to back up his three major arguments. His side won the debate.

Jacob really knew how to advocate for himself, if he felt he needed that. He wanted to drop an AP Calculus class for a couple of different reasons. Once you sign up and enroll for that class, it's very difficult to change your schedule, but Jacob obtained a meeting with our principal and presented his arguments as to exactly what he wanted, and the principal agreed.

Jacob made friends pretty easily, though at times I'm sure he was challenged. He was the only deaf student at the time who was mainstreamed in all of our classes. His friends included a pair of sisters named Barry and Rosie, who were extremely close to him. Jacob was always actively involved with other students when he worked in small groups in the classroom.

There was one incident when Jacob walked into class late, I believe it was from gym. When students walk into my class late, they either bring a pass or a short verbal excuse. Jacob walked over and spent about five minutes explaining why he was late: why it was hard to get his clothes changed, why it was hard to get to the classroom, why it was crowded in the hallway, and why he had to go to the restroom. I found it interesting how he had to go into all the intricacies and details of why he was late. The other students paid close attention as well, watching Diana try to interpret all of it.

At our high school, we hold auditions for graduation speeches. They're evaluated by a group of four or five teachers. There could be as many as eight to ten speakers auditioning. Jacob was one of them. After the auditions, we narrow it down to about four or five speakers for the actual graduation, and Jacob was one of the few selected. He signed his speech and had another student interpret and read it. It was a great success.

> **"To make our way we must have firm resolve, persistence, and tenacity We must gear ourselves to work hard all the way. We can never let up."**
> *Ralph Bunche*

Jacob, from day one, was always a challenge for me. I consciously wanted to face him all the time. Occasionally, if I tried to move around the classroom, my movement would be limited. Some of my videos were challenging, so I wanted them all subtitled so Jacob could understand. Some videos weren't subtitled, or were insufficient in their subtitles. I found that other students appreciated the subtitles as well, so I continue to turn them on for the ease of students who use them.

According to the 2011 American Community Survey, roughly eleven million people consider themselves deaf. Deaf people, as a culture, are richly diverse, and today they are making strides in every field. They're lawyers, CEOs, politicians and teachers. They're revolutionizing the idea of accessibility for everyone and everything.

Jacob went on to the National Technological Institute for the Deaf in Rochester, New York, for his first year of college. He continued his education and graduated from Gallaudet in Washington D.C. and obtained his degree in accounting. Currently, he works for an accounting firm in D.C.

At the end of every class, Jacob always signed a 'thank you' as he left the room. At this time, I would like to say to Jacob and Diana, a 'thank you' as well, for making me a better teacher. •

"Shantel, that is absolutely the cutest yellow dress I've ever seen, but what I really like is that yellow ribbon in your hair."

I often look back at Shantel's story and always reflect. Did I move fast enough? Could I have recognized the situation sooner? What are the clues that I missed? Maybe it was because it was my second year of teaching. Maybe I was naïve.

I first met Shantel in the gym on the very first day of school. All the students were sitting in the stands. I had my 6th-grade class roster, and when I read my class list, the students were supposed to line up in front of me. The first name that I read was Shantel's.

She came to me with a huge smile that I'll never forget.

After the class was in order, we went to the classroom where they were introduced to the room. One of the things that I always did, early in my career, was to purchase pencil boxes so that each student had their own utensils. Their pencil box included crayons, colored pencils, scissors, red and blue pens, a protractor and glue. Those would be the supplies they would use throughout the year.

Shantel was always positive; she always came in with a bright smile. I remember she was a great student. She was always inquisitive and prepared, turned in her assignments, and volunteered answers. Every day she came with a different, well kept, cute outfit. I could tell she cared a lot about how she presented herself. She was a fabulous little girl.

I recall a certain incident from back then. Even 45 years ago, I would always start my class with current events. I would sit in front of the class on a wooden stool and begin discussing relevant topics going on in the world. This particular time, while I was doing the current events, I guess I became so passionate and that my stool started shaking, then BOOM! I crashed onto the floor. When I hit the floor, I had 30 sixth graders laughing and wondering what was happening. There I was, sitting on the floor, and when I looked up, I saw Shantel standing over me. She was the very first child to help me. "Mr. Unger, can I help you up?" I'll never forget that.

One of the requirements for my students was to keep a journal. I bought them all notebooks to complete an entry each morning when they arrived in class and before they left every afternoon. Shantel would always take her time while she worked on her entries. She couldn't be rushed because it had to be perfect. She even took the time to draw a picture of a flower, or a kitten or a rainbow, something like that, to go along with her entry.

Because we were a self-contained class, most days I would eat with the students. When it was time to go to recess, some times I would sit with my class and chat. Many times I would sit with Shantel, and we'd talk about a variety of things. During our recess period, I'd play kickball with the kids, and I thought Shantel was very good at it, and clearly, she loved every moment of it.

One morning after Shantel came in and she had completed her journal entry, she asked, "Mr. Unger, can I take my pencil box home? I wanna do some drawing at home." I answered, "Sweetheart, absolutely! In fact, if you want you can keep it at home. I have some extras here at school you can have." She thanked me and flashed that wonderful smile. At that time, I would never have imagined the pain she had been having.

It was later on in the year, and I guess,being a new teacher with the same 30 students every day, I got to know them really well. I started to notice some subtle changes with Shantel. Sometimes, she'd be a little late to school, or her assignments were unfinished. She would even wear some of her outfits two days in a row. She still had a smile, she was still eager, but little things stood out to me. As time went on, these things became more noticeable, and I grew somewhat concerned. Seeing all of this, I decided to make a home visit.

During my time as a teacher, I've made over 350 home visits. When I planned these, sometimes I'd call to inform the parent that I'd like to come over and chat about how their child was doing in class; other times I'd go unannounced. Ninety-nine percent of the time I wanted to tell the parent something positive about their child. Very seldom was something ever negative. However, I was concerned about Shantel, and I thought it was necessary to make a visit. Sometimes when I'd tell a student I was coming over to their house, they'd dare me to show up.

"Mr. Unger, you're not coming to my neighborhood, you wouldn't dare come to my house." Then I'd say, 'I'll tell you what, when you get home and walk through the door, I'll bet you I'm talking to your mother in the living room."

"Mr. Unger, you wouldn't do that!"

"Watch me!"

Usually when I got to a neighborhood, I would circle it once to get a feel for the place before I parked, or I would double check to make sure that I had the right house. One time, during a home visit, I got out of my car and a student came up to me, shouting,

"Mr. Unger, Mr. Unger. What are you doing here?"

I said, "I'm here to visit one of my students."

"Okay, I'll wait for you to come back when you're done."

After I had finished my visit and came back, that old student of mine was sitting on my car. I asked,

"What are you doing?"

"Oh, Mr. Unger, I just want to talk to you," he replied.

Later on, I learned he was protecting my car. This kind of thing happened from time to time during my visits, so I learned not to question it.

So, I decided to make a visit to Shantel's house. It was at Dunbar Manor, and I had to walk about 50 yards down a grassy area to get to the apartment. As I was walking, more of my former students noticed me and they came up and asked,

"Hey, Mr. Unger, what are you doing here, are you visiting somebody?"

"Yes," I replied.

"We'll wait for you to come back, then we can catch up."

"That's fine."

I walked down towards the house, knocked on the door and noticed that the blinds in the apartment were moving. Despite this, I got no response. I knocked again. Still nothing. I decided to leave.

When I got back to my car, I invited the two guys who had been watching my car, to go out for lunch, as I was still unable to shake that uneasy feeling I had about Shantel.

The next day, I thought, *I'm gonna try this again, but this time, I'll call.* I tried to call a couple of times, **but there was still no answer.**

I decided to check Shantel's journal. I figured there was a chance she might have written some clues about what was going on at home. When I checked her journal, the first thing I noticed was that the entries were shorter. Instead of having a couple of sentences, sometimes it was just a phrase. I also saw that there were some blank pages, mostly in the morning. There were also fewer drawings with less color. When I'd sit with her during lunch, I had found her to be more withdrawn, which concerned me.

What did I do? I contacted the nurse. I had a great relationship with the nurse at that school, so I went to her and said,

> **"I want to send you a girl in my class. Her name is Shantel, and I'm going to tell her I need her to deliver something to you. When she gets there, I'd like you to try to see if there's anything that might be wrong, something that I'm missing."**

Less than half an hour later, the nurse showed up at my door and said gravely,

> **"Unger, Shantel's gone."**

> **"Excuse me?"** I said

> **"I called downtown and had a talk with the principal,"** she explained, **"and Children's Services came and got her right away."**

> **"Children's Services?"**

> **"Unger, she's been raped."**

She had been assaulted time and time again. It had started a while back. Her mother had been trafficking her the whole time, several times a week, and sometimes even several times a night.

I was shocked.

This beautiful, charming little girl with a wonderful smile and a yellow dress and ribbons in her hair had been living in hell.

Shantel was taken out of her house, and her mother and brother were arrested. Shortly thereafter, she was placed in a really good foster home, but she never came back to the school where I taught. However, I did make time to visit her with the permission from Child Protective Services. I even sat in a counseling session with her once or twice.

Later on in the spring, Shantel was doing well as far as I could tell. I was at school teaching my class. My room was on the bottom floor and behind me were the windows. The windows were about three feet off the ground, so someone could stand outside and look into the room. On that particular day, it was incredibly nice outside, so I had the windows open. As I was teaching, I noticed the students' eyes start to look behind me. I turned and saw a young man standing at the window. I approached the window, and asked, "Can I help you?"

He looked at me with a puzzled expression on his face.

"You're not supposed to be here," I continued, "this is school property—"

He looked at me and said, "You're the one."

He leaned in and took out a knife. He slashed right at my chest, and I jerked back about two feet. He cut my clothes but just barely nicked me. Had I not jumped back so quickly, I don't know what would've happened.

Later on, I found out that he had also been next door to another teacher's classroom first. When he looked in, he said, "You're the one," and he did cut that teacher.

"My mission in life is not merely to survive, but to thrive, and to do so with some passion, some compassion, some humor, and some style."
Maya Angelou

We all experience traumatic experiences in our lives. I'm sure there are girls and boys in my class right now, who are going through different kinds of hardships. Some trauma that we face can be physical pain, and injury, or an illness. Some adults have faced war, and their children have had to deal with the parent going to that war. Sometimes we experience natural disasters or acts of terrorism. A child could have experienced a death of someone close in the family, like a parent or a sibling—even a family pet. Some witness domestic abuse.

Rape is unthinkably traumatic.

She was a twelve-year-old girl.

People can respond to these events very differently. People can have nightmares, trouble sleeping or they can become very anxious or fearful Their mood can begin to shift. Some people become more irritable or angry. There can be depression or feelings of hopelessness. They can withdraw from the world or isolate themselves: this is what I saw with Shantel.

Managing your trauma response can be difficult. I believe the best way to cope is to spend time with others, communicate with family and friends, to try to eat regularly and stick to a routine. The counselor Shantel worked with recommended something along these lines when they were working together, trying to get her to open up to others again.

I went to Shantel's high school graduation. I took a dozen yellow roses with me. They were the same shade as that cute yellow dress and ribbons that she wore the first time we met. When I saw her, I told her, "Shantel, you are so strong. Congratulations on your graduation. Stay strong."

Shantel went on to graduate from Wright State University with a degree in nursing. She is currently a nurse in the Ohio area.

I often wonder and question myself. If I had not been such a young teacher, could I have recognized the signs sooner? Maybe the trauma wouldn't have happened if I had acted sooner.

Shantel, you taught me to be more observant, to be aware of subtle behaviors that are often masked. Teaching is not just about a student's academic ability, it is about the whole person. •

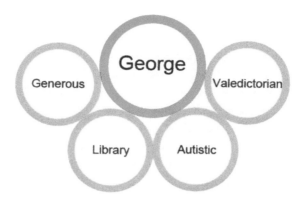

The first thing George said to me as he entered my sixth grade class was, "I want to sit at the front of the class. Is that okay?" He said this in a very deliberate and slow manner as if he were measuring every word. George was special and unique from the start. I never had a label for him; I knew that he saw the world differently. He paid attention to every detail in the classroom. His locker was arranged just so. The supply box I gave to each student contained colored pencils, crayons, a protractor and other typical items that students need on a daily basis. Unlike the other students, George had everything in that box arranged in a way that was never to be altered. Every paper he turned in had his name, date and subject in exactly the same place. When George pointed to his watch, showing me the time, I knew that the particular subject material in our self-contained classroom should be ending. He was so observant he even knew where I parked my car each day. One morning, when he exited the bus, he noticed a change. He came to me and said, "Mr. Unger, why did you change your parking spot?" I had only moved my car over one space to the right. "I just wanted to see if you'd notice."

Over time, I came to realize that George had a real gift for writing. He and one of the girls in the class were in charge of the class newspaper that we published on Fridays for the students to take home. The paper had school calendar updates, summaries of the different objectives for the week and a poem that George usually wrote. His poems usually had a theme of kindness. Each day I begin class with a discussion of current events. One day there was an article in the city newspaper that told of someone in Kroger's who had left $15 to help the next person in line help pay for their groceries. "Now that is called paying it forward," I announced to the class. "That's an act of kindness."

The woman who was the recipient of this good deed wanted to know who would do such a thing and choose to remain anonymous. Without any hesitation, but in his slow monotone voice, George spoke up, "That was me, Mr,. Unger."

At first the class and I were speechless. I clapped once and then I suddenly hesitated, the rest of the class responded similarly, and then all of us began to clap at once,

"Surely the woman would like to know what you did," I told George. "Are you in?"

Being George, he hesitated, and then he humbly asked, "Do you think it'd be okay?"

George continued, "You know, Mr. Unger, kindness is what reminds me of what's gotten me this far and what's possible to do for others."

I contacted Kroger's the next day, and a couple of days later, a representative from Kroger's and the lady who was the recipient of George's kindness, both came to our class to meet George. They gave George a Kroger's tee shirt, and a 'thank you'. George didn't want anything else. George also didn't show much emotion over that fuss either—in fact, he was really laid back.

One day after school, I made an unannounced home visit to George's. He wasn't home yet. While we were waiting for him, his mother and I had an informal chat in the living room for about 20 minutes. On the coffee table that was in the middle of the living room, George had a display of about 50 World War II army soldiers and some jeeps and tanks. As a kid, I used to have different sets much like his, such as a farm, Knights of the Round Table and Fort Apache. I used to spend endless hours arranging and rearranging them. I still have one of my old farm sets at home with all of the animals, the barns, the fencing and the tractors. If a child were to come over to my home today, I'd drag it all out, and the old memories would come rushing back to me.

I asked George's mother, "What would happen if I changed the position of just two of his pieces?" "Oh, as soon as he walks through the door he'll know." "May I?" I asked. She nodded in approval, but I could tell she had some questions. When George entered the living room, he didn't even make eye contact with me. He went straight to the table and fixed his plastic figures to adjust them as they had been.

After sixth grade, George continued his education at another public middle school. I kind of lost track of him, although I often worried about him, but figured he'd be okay. He eventually got a job at a local public library in his neighborhood. One day he came to see me to ask for a favor. "It's 'Banned Book Week' in the United States. Would you volunteer for a half-hour and read for us at the library?" "I'd be honored," I responded. "Can I choose what I want to read?"

I chose *The Things They Carried* by Tim O'Brien. I told George that I had my own autographed copy. When I arrived at the library, George introduced me to his supervisor. To read the book, I sat on a stool in the middle of a huge caged in area, while about 15 parents and students surrounded me. I read the very important first chapter to my listeners.

"Courage and perseverance have a magical talisman before which difficulties disappear and obstacles vanish into the air."
John Quincy Adams

Years later, I received another surprise visit from George. This time he invited me to his high school graduation where he was the Valedictorian giving the primary speech. The theme of his speech was autism and how different people deal with it. Autism Spectrum Disorder (ASD) is a developmental disorder that can cause significant social, communicative and behavioral challenges. There are usually no physical attributes that set the autistic person apart from others. However, ASD may affect a person in the way they interact, behave, learn and communicate. An autistic person can range from being gifted to severely challenged. Those who are challenged may have a language delay, or they may repeat words or phrases. Their awareness may be slower but not the ability to respond.

ASD affects every race, ethnic group and socio-economic background, but boys are four times more likely than girls to have the disorder. The Center for Disease Control (CDC) estimates that one out of every fifty-four children in the United States have been identified as ASD. Their ability to communicate and use of language depends on their individual intellectual and social development. People who are gifted tend to have rich vocabularies. They can express themselves with great detail, especially if the subject material is interesting to them. They will take endless time to prepare and they may be able to deliver an in-depth monologue on a specific topic. Musical talent or advanced mathematical ability is not unusual. Approximately ten percent of autistic children excel at memorization and music.

During his speech, George spoke to his audience with an intent to educate them. He concluded with a quote from the book *NeuroTribes: The Legacy of Autism and the Future of Neurodiversity* by Steve Silberman:

> *"Autism and other mental disorders should be seen as naturally human and not as defects."*

George accompanied by his mother and sister caught me at the end of the graduation program, to say: "Thank you, Mr. Unger, for believing in me to have my voice. Autism is an inspiration and not a disease. It's another way off looking at the world. You, Mr. Unger, saw that in me?" •

Ms. Taylor Kingston is the coordinator of the Creative Writing Department. She and her staff organized a poetry slam for the high school and middle school students. There were ten participants from the high school and four from the middle school and Karah was one of those high school poets. I approached Karah after she had performed and said,

> "I would really like to congratulate you on your beautiful spoken word. My name is Mr. Unger. I teach the Government class here at school."

> "I know who you are, Mr. Unger," Karah exclaimed. "My two older brothers had you as a teacher."

> "I didn't know they had a younger sister," I said.

> "Yeah, Mr. Unger. They were both adopted, and I'm adopted as well. I am the youngest in my family," Karah explained.

> "Could you please make some time in the next couple of days to come to my class during lunch because I would really like to get to know you more, after what you read?"

She was more than happy to visit with me, and as we sat across from each other, I asked her,

> "Karah, 'The Garden We Grow', where did you get this idea for your poem?" "I am passionate about my writing. If at least one person resonates with my ideas, then I know I've made a difference," said Karah. "I've had some depression

Karah

and anxiety issues, and I love to write. Putting pen to paper helps me express my feelings."

Karah suffers from anxiety and depression issues. Students face enormous pressures from family issues, from peers, from testing in schools, family issues, social media and cell phone usage. Anxiety is more common than many people realize and effects teenagers from all backgrounds. Excessive irritability, trouble sleeping, weight loss and weight gains, a sudden drop in grades and a sudden loss of interest in activities are all signs of anxiety and depression.

When Karah returned to my classroom to recite her poem in front of my class, she read her poem with such passion that she was met with a standing ovation.

The Garden We Grow
They tried to bury us
But they didn't know they planted seeds
Rooted in the soul
Clinging to the minerals
That we need

Sturdy we are
Growing we are
Breathing we are
Lungs

For the growing vines
symbol of our revolutionary designs

Come taste the sweetness
The divine glory of everlasting change
From now on
Our fruits will no longer be strange

Breathe in breathe out
Brace yourself to get drenched
At the end of this drought
Because prophecies come
In different amounts

A butterfly and pollen
The draft that's calling

For
Things to shift
To the calming breeze of
Sturdy trees
Activism is a gift

Where branches
Grown in generations

Pumping oxygen into
The winds of revolution
Waiting for justice to rain down
On broken institutions

Emerging like roses
From the ground
Except equipped with thorns
This time around

From Maya Angelou
To the Greensboro sit in
To Kamala Harris
Mrs. Vice President

To quote
A legacy was planting
Seeds in a garden you never get to see
In other words
We are writing our own history

As we thrive
We will not even apologize
Ancestors and stories retold
And inspiring declarations
Are contributions we hold

In other words make an impact
While you still have a chance
Scream, write, clap, shout
And you will change the world
Without a doubt

And these delicate flowers
Of everlasting beauty
Are seeds
That blossom
Starting with you and me

"Karah, a lot of things are going to come your way. Your current
ability to deal with adversity will equip you well for your future. Ms.
Kingston has helped you utilize your writing gift, and you, in turn, have

been able to use it as a platform to tell your story. Just know that during this time, this semester, this year, your family, friends and teachers, all support you. Karah, your garden is beautiful."

> "Freedom is a strong seed planted in a great need. I live here, too. I want freedom just as you.
>
> *Langston Hughes*

The Strength of Tenacity

Richard • Carlos • Dani • Justin • Ivory

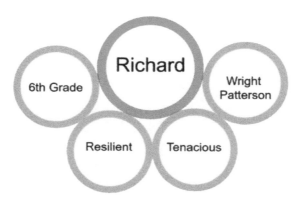

Richard was standing outside my door one day. But that's not where I should start this story. In the early 70s, I was teaching at Whittier Elementary school in west Dayton. It was a K-8 school with a population of about 500 students, mostly an African American population. The staff was mixed, but the students were not. At that time, the United States Justice Department decided the Dayton Public Schools were not integrating quickly enough, so the district decided to use forced bussing. Several strategies had failed, so the final plan was to pair the highly African American schools from one side of town and bus them to the more dominantly white schools on the other side of town. Whittier was paired with a school across town with a 98 percent white population. I don't know what formula they used to decide on this plan, nor do I know how they determined which students would remain in their home school or which ones would leave. However, half of Whittier would be bussed to the majority white school and half of the majority white school would be bussed to Whittier. After one year, the populations would be switched, and the other half who had stayed in their home schools, would be bussed over, while the first half would stay in place.

I cannot begin to talk about the reaction that this generated within the city, because nobody was pleased. Even if they were satisfied one year, the following year, their child would have to move to an entirely different school. Every parent was upset and passionately so.

Doug Jeffries, another teacher at Whittier, and I, made visits to the exchange school during the first year so that we could introduce ourselves and make the transition easier. Whittier's principal at that time, encouraged this, and it worked out well.

When school began in the fall, I had 35 students in my classroom. I had no idea who was black or white based on the class list. When I walked on the first day, I found the class was pretty well split, both in race and gender. Was it a challenge? Sure, why wouldn't it be? I had kids I knew, and kids I didn't know, and they were all trying to get along with each other. Did we work it out? Yeah, after several weeks, it was fantastic. I had a self-contained classroom of sixth graders, who had all managed to adapt to the new circumstances.

After about the first two weeks though, I noticed there was a student lurking in the hallway, a young white child with short brown hair, and he'd just stand there. I have always taught with my door open, regardless of the age group. It was fairly easy for this student to listen in, and for me not to notice him. Each time I went toward him, he would leave, so I never had the chance to talk to him. At first, I didn't worry since I had my own class to teach, and they were my priority. Nevertheless, this continued to happen over the course of several days. I would be teaching, and he would be standing there. It seemed like he'd been scoping out my class for a while.

Finally, he stayed when I walked up to him, and we talked. I began to introduce myself, and the first thing he said was, **"I know who you are. You're Mr. Unger."**

I asked, "And you are?"

"My name's Richard, I wanna be in your class. I've been watching your class, and I want to be in your class. I don't

want to be in the Special Ed class that I've been assigned to, and I don't belong there."

"I have no control over that," I responded. "I mean, if you've been assigned to that class because of testing, or whatever, I can't just change classes on a whim like that."

And he said, "I have to be in your class. And I'm not leaving."

"Oh yeah you are," I said.

I called the principal who took Richard back to his class; however, on the following day, he was back, standing outside again and refusing to leave. Finally, we went to the principal together, called parents and test administrators, and eventually, Richard was assigned to my class.

Richard stayed for the rest of the year, and he did a great job. He wasn't an A+ student, but he turned everything in and worked hard. He fit in well, and he got along well.

At the end of the year, it's very hard to say goodbye to the students, especially in a self-contained class, where it's like a family. When the time came, Richard walked up to me, and he said, **"Unger, thank you, I really needed you to be my teacher."**

> "Your life's work is to find your life's work and then to exercise the discipline, tenacity, and hard work it takes to pursue it."
> *Oprah Winfrey*

I replied to him, **"Richard, it works both ways."**

And so we hugged each other and said goodbye; I didn't see him again until 2018.

I was in my classroom, grading some papers and I received a phone call. I picked the phone up, and the first thing I heard was, **"Mr. Unger, you probably won't remember me, but my name is Richard."**

"Could it be Richard T.?"

"Yeah, Mr. Unger, you remember me?"

I said, "Yeah, Richard, I remember you. You were the one who stood outside my classroom for about two weeks, wanting to be in my class. Of course, I remember you."

"I watched your class for the longest time. I had to be in your room. Can we get together to talk about some things I want to say?"

We met at the Dublin Pub, and we had some drinks and dinner, and we talked for the longest time. For the most part, we were catching up, and as we were sharing stories, I forgot most things, while Richard seemed to remember everything. He told me he had interned at Wright Patterson Air Force Base while in high school and that he was still working there when we met. When we were finished, he said to me, "Unger, I want you to know you saved my life. I didn't belong in that classroom. I need to say 'thank you.'"

I almost didn't know what to say.

We stay in touch, and every once in a while, we'll check up on each other. I think there's a lesson here to be learned. As a teacher, one of the things I've learned in all of my years is that the characteristic I admire the most in a student is tenacity, someone who is willing to see a job through and be tenacious. Richard, standing outside my door, and not taking 'no' for an answer, was as tenacious as he could be. To me, I think that tenacity is the most critical attribute for achievement. Tenacity is more important than intelligence. I'm not putting intelligence down, but tenacity is more important. Great, successful people are tenacious and willing to get the job done. You aren't born with it, but you develop tenacity by setting goals, always re-evaluating and checking your attitude, and being able to deal with both success and failure. You have to be able to take action and do something, and embrace failure when it comes, but you have to keep going all the time. Never give up, never surrender. I just want to thank you, Richard, for your tenacity. ●

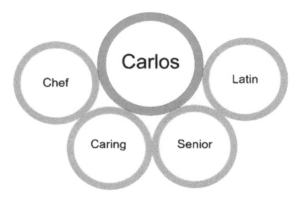

One day after class, Carlos was getting ready to walk out, and I asked him if he wanted to do some work on a Saturday. A friend of mine was moving out of his house, and he had so much junk that I needed some strong backs to help, and I figured some of my students might like to have a little extra money. Carlos said he would.

Carlos was a senior in my American Government class, and he was a good student. His parents are from Mexico, and he is the first generation here in America. He'd often translate for his parents during meetings; he always paid attention in the classroom; he always turned his assignments in on time, and he was very active in class in a positive way.

I asked him once, probably around November, if he had any idea what he was going to do after high school. He said he already pretty much knew, since his dad had told him. I asked him what that would be, and he said,

"My dad said I'll be on the roof."

"You'll be up on the roof?"

"Unger, you look puzzled. That means I'll be doing roofing, since my father works for a roofing company."

"But you have a lot of other things going on, I said. You could apply to college and get in. Your GPA is good, you're a bright young man—"

"Mr. Unger, my father pretty much said I'm gonna be up on the roof."

I asked him what he did after school, and he told me that he has to cook and care for his siblings.

Eventually, the day came around to help my neighbor move. I picked up Carlos and five other young men from their homes. After we worked out what we would pay them, we spent about three and a half to four hours working. We cleaned out the whole basement and threw everything into a huge dumpster.

When I took the kids home, I specifically saved dropping Carlos off for last. Just before he got out of the car, he turned to me and said,

> **"Mr. Unger, when I turn eighteen in January, my parents are kicking me out." I said, "Wait a minute. What do you mean they're kicking you out."?**

> **"Well, my father doesn't think I put in enough time on the weekends helping him out. He's upset with me, and they're gonna kick me out of the house. When I turn eighteen, they don't want me anymore."**

> **"Who's gonna babysit your brothers and sisters? Who's gonna take care of them?"**

> **"I don't know, Mr. Unger. I don't know. But they're gonna kick me out," he said. "I wanna stay in school and graduate."**

> **"Can I intervene?" I asked. "Can I talk to your parents? Can I make a home visit?"**

> **"You can, but it's not gonna do any good. He's pretty much made up his mind that if I'm not gonna do what he want me to do, then I'm out of there."**

> **"Well, maybe we can work out some kind of compromise, where you still work some of the time, but you can get other things done as well."**

> **"Mr. Unger, my dad doesn't compromise too much."**

Homelessness is a huge problem in our country. One in thirty adolescents, ages 13-17, face some form of homelessness. Homelessness can be caused by family rejection: it's not usually based on sexual orientation or gender identity, it doesn't have to be based on any thing specific, and Carlos' family just decided that he had to leave. Fifty percent of homeless youths end up unsheltered and sleeping outside, and it's always because of some unresolved family conflict.

> **"It takes courage to grow up and become who you really are."**
> *e.e.cummings*

To end homelessness, youth and young adults need suitable housing with supportive conditions and caring adults. These young people must have access to mainstream services that will place them back on a path to success. However, the key problem is in trying to attempt a reunification between the homeless young person and his/her family.

I finally decided to visit Carlos' home to attempt an intervention as his teacher. His mother didn't want to kick out Carlos, but his father was persistent. Together, we worked out a compromise that could possibly make something different happen. Regardless of what I had believed was possible, in January I had a call from a pay phone, and it was Carlos. His father had kicked him out.

I asked Carlos where he was and I picked him up and brought him to my home. I fixed him some food. My wife and I sat down for a while, and we agreed to allow Carlos to stay with us on a temporary basis, with the objective that he would be able to return to his home.

Carlos ended up staying for a week. We were able to become acquainted in a different way, and it was really a great time. I asked him to fix dinner one night, and he made black bean soup and burritos that were just incredible! Carlos was really a good cook. I could see why his siblings wanted him back home.

We finally worked out a new compromise to get Carlos back home. Weekends he would work with his father, but weekdays he would be allowed to do his school work. Nevertheless, at the end of the school year, during the last week of school, Carlos was still working with his dad. I ended up taking Carlos down to Sinclair Community College to introduce him to the Admissions Officer. Carlos filled out an application for admission as well as one for financial aid. He worked out any schedule issues that he might have. After one year, Carlos transferred to Ohio State, and he majored in mechanical engineering. When he graduated from the university, he invited me to his ceremony, and of course I went.

In Dayton, we have a great program called *Daybreak*, located downtown at 605 South Patterson Boulevard. *Daybreak* is staffed twenty-four hours a day, seven days a week and it is open to youths from 10-21. There is the capacity to house 24 youths with single bedrooms, private baths, three meals daily, in addition to personal care and clothing. The agency has high security, and they work to reconnect children and youth to their home. *Daybreak* is just one resource amidst a group that provide for homeless young people.

Did I think about *Daybreak* for Carlos? Yes, but at that time, it was full, which is why I took him to my home. One thing we talked about together when he was undergoing the crisis, was that he should never feel guilty or blame himself because he was a homeless teen. I assured him that he was not alone and that he could always ask me for help.

I thank you, Carlos, for telling me that you needed help, because you opened my eyes to a segment of society that I needed to see, and this made it a worthwhile experience. Carlos told me, **"Mr. Unger, if it wasn't for you, I probably would be up on the roof today. I can't thank you and your wife enough."**

We hugged and laughed. We still keep in touch with each other. Last time I saw him, I said, **"Carlos, pay it forward to someone else."** •

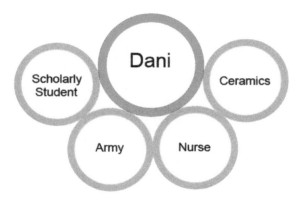

"Dani, have you decided on your plans for next year after graduation? Have you thought about where you would like to be next year at this time." This is where our story begins, with a question that is simple to ask, but for some students it is a struggle to answer. It starts in a classroom decorated with posters, a collage of different magazine articles, posters designed to empower people, each with their own story to be told. This story starts at the beginning of every year, when David Asadorian, an amazing school counselor, asks me if he can come in and talk to seniors about their post-graduation plans.

October is about the time when I start asking students about their plans for the future: what field of study they might be considering or what type of career they might wish to pursue. Some students immediately know while others have no idea what they want to do. I tell them that *not* knowing everything about their future is 'okay.' After all, the future that is in front of them is greater than the time they have already lived. They need to keep their options open, to be aware of the possibilities. I also tell them that if they need recommendations, I'll be happy to write some for them.

Our counselor, Mr. Asadorian, will come in and talk about testing dates for college entrance exams and due dates for college applications, both critical for those who intend to go to college. He'll take a good twenty or thirty minutes to talk about the Free Application For Student Aid (FAFSA) which is a program where seniors can apply for their federal aid for scholarships. Additionally, David will discuss other scholarship opportunities as well as a variety of job opportunities and career paths that are available for students who are not going on to college. Included in this discussion are trades that are trying to recruit graduating seniors. Finally, he goes over the military options that are available after high school and the differences between the branches of service.

Periodically, I'll bring in a military recruiter who is willing to talk to the students. I always expose them to the different branches, but I never try to 'sell' the military. I know from personal experience that it is not for everyone. Finally, he goes over the military options that are available after high school and the differences between the branch options.

I like discussing all options with my students. I tell them what "active duty" means, the obligations of the National Guard, and I even talk about the Reserve Officer Training Corp (ROTC). I have a little background with the military, so I have no reason to shy away from a discussion about the military as a career option. I was drafted into the Army after one year in college in 1970. My basic and advanced infantry training took place at Fort Leonard Wood and Fort Ord. My military occupation status was 11B (infantry). I was deployed overseas from 1971 to 1972 and came back as an E-5. I try to share my experience and provide general knowledge of the military with my students.

Danielle was a fabulous student in my class. Each day she had a positive attitude. She always finished her work, and she was an 'A' student. She had many friends, was in the Ceramics Magnet, and she was extremely talented. When I asked her about her postgraduate plans, she said she was going into the Army. I asked her to meet with me after school for about thirty-minutes to talk. I want to know the thinking of any student who chooses the military because I feel that I need to prepare them. I have always thought about my students in the same way that I have thought about my own child. I want what is best for each of them.

Although special measures are being taken now to combat sexual harassment in the Armed Forces, it is still an issue which concerns me. On the day Dani stayed after school to talk, we had a good discussion about her plans. I asked her why she had chosen the Army. She told me,

"I want to be a nurse, and I think that the Army could give me the best background," Mr. Unger.

"Why not the Navy? Why not the Air Force?" I wanted to know why she was choosing the Army over any of the other branches.

"I think the Army because some of my family was in the Army, and I want to go in that direction."

I was trying to get another reason for her Army choice. "Can't you go to college and then perhaps join the National Guard? Can't you apply for ROTC and then you will graduate as an officer, then enter the Armed Forces and pursue nursing?"

"No, Mr. Unger, I don't want any part of college because I really can't afford to pay for it, and I don't want my parents to do it. I don't want to feel obligated to them. So, I want to do this on my own and I think the Army is the best choice."

"Great. I think you made a great decision. Have you taken your ASVAB?"

(The ASVAB [Armed Services Vocational Aptitude Battery] is an aptitude test that measures developed abilities and helps predict future academic and occupational success.)

"I have and I scored pretty high."

"Because you scored high, what do you qualify for?"

"I'm going to be a 68W Combat Medic Specialist."

"Where are you going?"

"To Fort Sam Houston. Then for my advanced individual training, that'll be another 16 weeks, just for Medic."

"Sounds like you've done your background."

Throughout the year I would check up her, and once in a while I would ask, "How's your military situation going?"

She answered, "Well, I'm in training this weekend, and I'm going to be with my recruiter."

I continued to speak to Dani at different times during the balance of the year, and Dani would remain positive and continued with a positive attitude.

Upon her graduation, Dani enlisted immediately and she had a going away party. She invited me to her incredible party that her parents had hosted. Several of her classmates were there, and all were extremely proud of her, as I was.

Dani knew what she wanted to do. She wanted to be a nurse, and she was using the Army as a vehicle to get there. After she went through her basic and then advanced training, she was attached to the 82nd Airborne, and she was deployed to Afghanistan where she worked in the hospital. She faced a lot of problems. After her deployment, Dani visited Stivers. One day I found her standing at my door dressed in uniform, looking absolutely incredible. I was so proud of her. "I'm back in town, can we get together?" "Absolutely," I said.

When we met, we talked and I asked her, "So, what did you do?"

"Well, in the hospital, I didn't see too many of the guys in my unit."

The thing that really captured my attention was when she talked about the injured civilians.

"I'll probably never get over the images that I saw of the women, men and children."

"Sounds like you've done a lot."

"I want more."

"You want more?"

"Yes. When I was in Afghanistan, I worked in a hospital. I wanted to get out in the field with the men."

"Okay. You're 82nd Airborne which means you probably need to go to 'jump school'. You've got to go to Fort Benning, do

your parachute training and then, more than likely, you'll be assigned with those men."

And so she did.

"And one day she discovered that she was fierce, and strong and full of fire, and not even she could hold herself back because her passion burned brighter than her fears."
Mark Antony

She returned and volunteered at Fort Benning where she went to jump school. On her second tour, she was no longer part of the hospital scene, but out on the field with the men, where she had wanted to be.

When she returned from her second tour of duty, instead of discussing her encounters, we talked about the stories she wanted to share. Immediately thereafter, she enrolled at the Wright State University School of Nursing where she later graduated.

I saw her a year after she had enrolled in nursing school. Ms. Bridget Federspiel organized a program at Stivers, and we brought in a Congressional Medal of Honor Awardee, Sergeant Melvin Morris. Dani came back because she had heard that he was going to be a guest. When I saw Dani, I thought to myself, *wow, great to see you.* She had her partner with her, another veteran. As we talked, I discovered that she was still working on her nursing degree. I know that she is now a nurse somewhere in the Dayton area. We still text each other from time to time to keep up with one another.

Since I've been at Stivers, I would say that over 50 young men and women have gone into all the branches of the military after their graduation. They've all served with distinction and honor. Many have shown up unexpectedly at my classroom door. We hug and they want to talk. Because of their military duty, they usually want to shake my hand, but I always want a hug.

My concern lies with their return. There is a huge problem in America with Post Traumatic Stress Disorder (PTSD) as a result of their military experience. Thirty-thousand veterans, men and women, have committed suicide: 17-18 daily, and about 6,500 yearly. When I teach American History in my class, I like to teach about the "blackeyes" in our history: the issues that we still need to work on as Americans. One of these issues is our returning veterans. We are unable to save enough of them. These issues *can be* resolved.

Dani

More psychologists and sociologists must take the time with our returning heroes. The problem can be solved. First, we need to identify those persons who might need help with their readjustment to society: work and family issues; personal flashbacks; the tools that are available to help them adjust from their military experiences back into society. We need to provide our veterans with program availability that meets their psychological and personal needs. Wright State University, the University of Dayton and Ohio State University offer such programs with opportunities that can address our returning military.

Dani took advantage of these programs when she came home. She had found meaning in what she had done. She used her background to become a successful nurse. She completed her nursing program, and with that, she was able to re-adapt, and she is a contributing member of society.

When our warriors return home to become civilians once again, we must be aware of those who need help, and we must encourage those who need to complete their education.

"Let us remember the service of our veterans, and let us renew our national promise to fulfill our shared obligations to our veterans and their families who have sacrificed so much so we can live free."
Dan Lipinski

Dani, thank you for your service. •

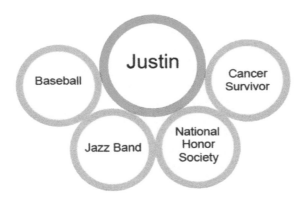

I often stand outside my classroom door between periods, but on one particular day, I hesitated to go back into class. As I turned, I caught Justin walking towards me. He looked so pale, returning from a chemotherapy appointment.

"I see you're right on time," I said to him. Justin returned with, "You know I try to be."

At this time, I was teaching freshmen, and all six classes were American History; Justin was in one of these. He was a multi-talented person. He played the trumpet in the jazz band, which had garnered several awards and played in competitions throughout the area. He also played first base on the baseball team. Justin was the kind of student who wanted to participate in multiple activities in academics, sports and the arts. By the time he graduated, he was in the National Honor Society, and he had taken many rigorous courses. He was an exceptional student.

In his freshman year, about three weeks into school, he was diagnosed with leukemia. Leukemia is a cancer that affects the body's blood forming tissues... it can include the bone marrow and the lymphatic system. It is the most common kind of cancer among children. It can be treated with chemotherapy, but it comes with the side effects of fatigue, nausea, appetite and hair loss.

Here was a 15-year-old young man, who had just started high school, trying to become involved with as many things as he could to acclimate himself into the high school scene, and right away he comes down with leukemia. His comment to me after he was diagnosed was,

"Will I be able to keep up?"

I tried to thoughtfully reply to him, "I don't know Justin, will you be able to keep up? I think you will. I see you walking down the hall each day after your chemo, and you're always in my class."

He didn't respond to me right away, so I repeated, "I think you'll be able to keep up."

Justin decided he wanted to make sure the rest of the freshman class knew what he was going through. He didn't put it out there, but he wanted to make sure they knew. The people he shared the basketball team with, the people he shared the jazz team with, the people he shared his classes with, all knew.

Throughout the next several months, he and I would have sit downs, and during these sit downs, we would discuss many of the challenges for a person with cancer. He basically had one conclusion, his life would never be the same. He also said that to survive he would need 'hope-makers', people who would inspire and guide him, to give him the support he needed.

Justin had to leave his old story behind, the one he knew before cancer, and create a new story. He understood at his young age that this was what he must do in order to survive and grow, he needed to create a new story. He needed to include new people in this story. This would help him survive.

Justin

Success! With all the tests and chemotherapy, he did survive. Justin went into remission during the late spring. The Dayton Dragons along with Dayton Medical Center hosted an event called, "A Home Run for Your Life." The Dragons invited Justin down to their field for a celebration of his life and beating cancer. Prior to the game, the opposing team lined up on the first base line, and the Dragons lined up on the third base line. Justin, with his family, went down to the home plate. The announcer told the audience his name and explained Justin's fight with cancer. At the conclusion of this announcement, Justin ran all of the bases. Applause filled the stadium as Justin ran from first base and headed to second. The entire crowd stood on their toes as the applause grew louder. As he rounded to third base, each of the Dayton Dragons gave him a 'high five,' while some reached out to hug him. When he arrived at the home plate, he waved to the sky and stared back at the roaring crowd. There weren't many in the stadium without tears in their eyes, and I'm sure Justin could feel their empathy and joy.

"Sports a metaphor for overcoming obstacles and achieving against great odds. Athletes, in times of difficulty, can be important role models!"
Bill Bradley

Justin survived cancer. He continued to attend Stivers for the balance of his high school years. He also continued to be an incredible student, and he participated in everything. I was invited to his graduation party where his family and a multitude of friends celebrated his accomplishments. He chose to attend Rose-Hulman Institute of Technology in Indiana, known for its prestigious engineering program, and Justin graduated in the 131st commencement in 2009 with his degree in Engineering.

> ## "You are braver than you believe, stronger than you seem, smarter than you think, and twice as incredible as you'd ever imagine."
> *Cancer Survivor*

Little did I know that 20 years later, Justin would become one of *my* primary teachers. I am going through the same thing Justin did. I have to find a new way of living. Life is not the same for me. All the conclusions that Justin came to, I am coming to now. I am writing a new story, but the greatest thing he taught me was to look toward the future. I have several great 'Hope-Makers,' but I'm still missing a few. Every cancer survivor has a story filled with fear, hope and courage, and although all survivors have many things in common, no two journeys are the same. All cancer stories can inspire the passion in all of us to keep on fighting.

Justin was a cancer survivor, and I will be a cancer survivor.

Thank you, Justin, for being a great role model and teacher. •

I was walking into Stivers one morning, a week before school started, on schedule preview day. Schedule preview day is when students come in before the beginning of the school year to review their schedules and figure out where their classes are going to be.

On this particular morning, I had tennis practice with the varsity girls' tennis team across the street from the school. I figured that I would simply stop into Stivers to look through my mailbox and quickly check up on a few things. I wasn't working the schedule preview day. I just wanted to just stop in and see how things were going.

As I walked into the school, I noticed a car parked in front with its windows down. I heard a voice from the car.

"Hey, sir, do you know who Mr. Unger is?"

Curious, I countered, "Who's asking?"

"My name is Ivory," replied the young man, "I just got my schedule and I see that I've got Mr. Unger for American History and I was just kind of curious as to who he is…"

At that time, I was teaching one class of freshman American History and five classes of senior American Government. Ivory was in my single American History class.

"Yeah…I know who he is. Just wait, you'll find out probably next week who he is." And so, a week later, we began a close friendship that's lasted over ten years.

"Persistence can change failure into extraordinary achievement"
Matt Biondi

Those of us who are successful urban teachers learn from our students *all* the time. One of the things I try to do daily, is to start my classes off with a discussion of the world's current events. I remember one time, when I was late coming from lunch to Ivory's class. As I was coming up the stairs, I heard someone in my classroom teaching in my short absence. Surprised, I did *not* walk in right away. I stood outside the door and eavesdropped. And there was Ivory, leading the current events for the day. He was also having fun mimicking me, because there was a lot of laughter coming from inside my room. He was mimicking my hand gestures, mimicking how I point and mimicking my speech. It was hilarious but informative—although a bit more hilarious than it was informative, I think. So, when I popped my head around the corner into the classroom, you could've heard a pin drop. Ivory was sitting on my stool in front of the class, a little bit embarrassed. My first comment was, "You seem to be doing a pretty good job. You've got a handle on that, Ivory! I think for the next two days, you'll be doing the current events!"

And sure enough, he had current events for the next two days and did a great job. I think, as teachers, we have to jump on teachable moments and allow ourselves to be a little bit vulnerable and see if students can rise to the occasion. Ivory always seemed to be able to do that.

I teach students history and government. However, my first priority is always the students. Whenever I can, I try to find moments where I can teach my students life lessons to get them prepared for the real world outside of my classroom. The students call it "real".

Ivory's accomplishments at Stivers, over the four years that he was there, were vast. He had great leadership skills. He was vice president of the Student Council, and he was part of the Optimist club. Although the school doesn't have this club any longer, when the Optimist club did exist, it would meet once a month, and a group of students would go downtown to a hotel in Dayton, have lunch, and hook up with a mentor. This mentor could be a veteran, business leader, lawyer, police person, fire person or a local politician. They would have lunch with the students and talk to them. During his high school career, Ivory worked very closely with the athletic director, taking tickets at games, and working the scoreboard during basketball games. He was very responsible in that way.

Ivory also played basketball on the freshman and sophomore teams: I went to many of his games during his freshman year. I always attend my students' athletic events and concerts so I can get to know them better as individuals rather than just students. The reason Ivory sat out basketball in eleventh grade was because his grades were poor, and he wanted to make sure his grades were good. So, he sacrificed basketball, which he would have played, and been a starter for the JV team. However, he came back and played his senior year. He was not a starter during his senior because of his gap year, but he did play a large supportive role on the team, and he enjoyed just being a team member.

At Stivers, Ivory was also in the choir, and he was a talented singer. The choir would sometimes perform outside of Stivers, and Ivory sang for a luncheon at Coco's Bistro, an upper-end restaurant in downtown Dayton named after the owners' daughter who also attended Stivers. At his last concert at Stivers, Ivory sang "Precious Lord" with the rest of the choir. Stivers' choir director was especially proud of the group because they expressed such passion during the song.

During his senior year, Ivory had the lead role in *Raisin in the Sun*, even though he wasn't a member of the theater department. However, Ivory wanted to audition, which was permissible, and he got the lead.

Ivory applied to his dream school, University of Kentucky after graduation, and he enrolled and majored in Music Education because he loved his music so much. He also wanted to take classes that would allow him to become a nurse. However, at the very beginning of the semester, Ivory had some financial problems, and he called me.

"Mr. Unger, I'm in trouble. I do not have all of my books or the money to get them... I'm really worried about this affecting my first year."

"Don't you worry about a thing, Ivory," I said, as I jumped in my car, picked him up, took him to the bookstore and bought all of the books he needed for his first semester.

He had a good first year, all things considered. He was a bit disappointed in the music program that they had to offer. His money issues also continued, so he transferred from the University of Kentucky back to Ohio to attend Sinclair Community College in Dayton. He stayed at Sinclair for a year to finish all of his general education courses and then he transferred to The Ohio State University. At Ohio State, he was a resident's assistant (RA) for two years, fostering community 'building' within the college. He majored in, of all things, Social Studies. He was training to be a teacher for the most part, so he dropped the idea of a music career, although he still loves to sing.

As soon as he graduated, he was a hot commodity. He currently works at the Metro College Middle and High School which is attached to Ohio State, teaching social studies for sixth through eighth grades. Currently, because of his attachment to Ohio State, he is also working on his Masters and PhD at Ohio State.

Ivory, you should be so proud of your incredible journey. It's only the beginning. •

Facing Insurmountable Odds

Sheldon • Lonnie • Chris

Sheldon said, "Now, Mr. Unger, we have even more in common than we did before? Sheldon was a student in my senior U. S. Government class in 2010, and let me tell you, what a student he was! Sheldon was a member of the orchestra and the theater department. In orchestra, Sheldon specialized in playing the oboe and the saxophone, and he was a phenomenal musician. Sheldon's theatrical journey started a bit after his orchestral endeavor. In his freshman year of high school, Sheldon decided to run track, but at the end of the season, he decided it was not for him, so he auditioned for the play, *Months on End*. After this first performance, Sheldon felt beckoned by the theater. He performed in numerous plays through the remainder of high school, and he was especially proud of his last performance in the play, *A Streetcar Named Desire*.

Sheldon was also in the Spanish Honors Society and in varsity wrestling he competed in the 175 pound weight class. When I rewatch some of Sheldon's matches, I am always caught off guard by a certain level of toughness that he illustrated even in his youth. Toughness seemed to be the most dominant trait that always remained integral to Sheldon, especially later in his life.

In the summer following his high school graduation, Sheldon invited me to the play, *Pick up the Pieces,* where he had the privilege of starring in the lead at Antioch College in Yellow Springs, Ohio. The play centered around several U.S. military personnel who were returning from overseas. Sheldon knew that I had always been passionate about veterans and their mental and physical hardships.

With the help of Mr. Asadorian, Sheldon applied for the Bill and Melinda Gates Scholarship where he was granted a full ride to any college of his choice. Sheldon decided to take his academic and acting skills to Emerson College in Boston, Massachusetts. He still loves Boston and often returns there to connect with old friends.

Sheldon's next stop was Chicago, where he has acted with the Goodman Theater, the Steppenwolf Group and the About Face Theater. Sheldon had a part in the play, *Choir Boy,* where the story line follows the 1919 Chicago race riots. Currently, Sheldon is rehearsing for his part in *Stephane's Reflection*, which follows the Gullah people of South Carolina's and the Gulf Coast's low country. Sheldon has acted in several movies, but he is most proud of his role in the film, *Cicada,* because he co-wrote the script and also had a lead role. The film was nominated for a Spirit Award, and Sheldon attended the awards ceremony in Los Angeles. Sheldon says he has made so many connections there, and he knows this is where he needs to be.

> ## "The biggest adventure you can take is to live the life of your dreams."
> *Oprah Winfrey*

In addition to his acting career in Chicago, Sheldon also teaches there. He is extremely proud of his teaching experiences where he has worked with the Northlight Theater Company, as well as in Evanston, for years. He conducts workshops in theaters, and Sheldon enhances his classes with the concept of relationship building. His students have the responsibility to create art pieces that celebrate and address a variety of community issues common to the area, and he challenges his students to create a 'conversation'. On that matter Sheldon told me, "Don't worry, Unger; your legacy continues with me. You made a difference with me; you taught me; and I like teaching my students. I want to make a difference in their lives."

Sheldon, actor and writer.

Sheldon and Michael Unger in Chicago.

Sheldon is staying politically active. He campaigned relentlessly for Hillary Clinton in 2016 and was disappointed with her loss. He is currently researching material about Ida B. Wells and the Southern Horror Lynch Law.

The toughness I noted in Sheldon during high school has still stayed with him. He related an experience he had in early April 2018, while he was walking home from a friend's birthday party on a Saturday night. It was just three blocks from the 'L' to his apartment. He was in the alley when a car pulled up beside him, and someone inside rolled down the window and asked the 25-year old where the party was. "Before I could answer, they just started shooting," he said. He heard three shots, and then he felt heat and pain radiating through his abdomen where one of the shots had landed. As the bullet tore through the abdomen, it fractured his pelvic bone and lodged in his opposite hip bone. Sheldon lay still on the sidewalk, playing dead, hoping the car would just drive away. When the car finally left, Sheldon tried to reach for his phone, but he was unable to move. When the police arrived, Sheldon was silent, and he said,

"I was just thinking, my mom passed away when I was younger; my grandmother passed away in my junior year in high school, and so I was talking to them. I'm not ready to see you just yet mom, grandma. God, I don't want to go out like this."

Sheldon's roommate and friend, Peter, helped him [Sheldon] through therapy and helped him with a lot of his hospital bills. "He was always there for me." Peter reported that Sheldon would frequently converse with the nurses, and one time Sheldon joked, "This is my first and hopefully my last time seeing all of you: I'm not a cat with nine lives."

Once the major surgeries had been completed, I called the hospital where I was finally put through to Sheldon's room. A nurse who had picked up the room's phone, cautiously asked for my last name. "My name is Michael Unger, I'm one of Sheldon's former teachers, is he available?" The nurse kind of hesitated and answered, "Well, I don't know if he's available. Can I ask again, who's calling?"

When I repeated my name again, I could hear Sheldon's impatient voice, "Give me the phone. I want to talk to him."

In our last moments of that conversation, Sheldon retorted, "You know Unger, now we've got even more to talk about. You were shot on the streets of Dayton, and I was shot on the streets of Chicago."

During that same weekend, Sheldon and 23 others were wounded, and two people were killed because of gun violence in the streets of Chicago. Sheldon was just one of the nameless victims, identified as "...a 25-year-old man [who was] taken to Illinois Masonic Hospital in good condition…" No arrest was ever made in the shooting.

Sheldon told me,

> "Someone shot me, and he looked just like me. I don't want to be the person that is living my life through hate and vengeance. Living in this world as a Black is dangerous because you're constantly living in a realm of uncertainty, I want to be able to allow people to see us and see us as human beings. And hear us and hear our voices. That is the work I want to do. That is the work that I've been blessed to do, and the work I will continue doing here in Chicago."

Following his months in the hospital and rehab, Sheldon traveled to Los Angeles for an audition. He acted in a film in New York and appeared in the production, *This Bitter Earth,* at the About Face Theater. Sheldon related to me and emphasized that to be able to walk again and to say, "This is who I am, and this is my body," is a beautiful thing. He continued talking about wanting to walk about the world and say,

> "Here I am. Here I am! I can't live in a state where people are making me feel like I don't belong. Of course, I belong because I was shot and I survived and I'm alive. I belong… There was a reason I survived the shooting. I don't think it was so I could live my life in fear, but to actually go and be further driven to the things I was called to do.
>
> Fear can cripple and prevent a person from living, and it can motivate. I choose the latter," said Sheldon.

So, I asked Sheldon, "What did you learn from your experience?"

> "It allowed me to dig deeply into my own humanity. If you love yourself deeply and others deeply, you can grow from any encounter. I remember when I was in the hospital, you said, 'You have to own the trauma, and count on the love and support from those friends and family.'" He went on to

say. "I wasn't about to let the dream die, Unger. I feel like I'm just getting started."

"We don't even know how strong we are until we are forced to bring that hidden strength forward. In times of tragedy people do amazing things. The human capacity for survival and renewal is awesome."
Isabel Allende

The year after the shooting, in 2019, Sheldon was invited to his Alma Mater, Emerson College to give a speech. Emerson awarded Sheldon "The President's Award for Creative Courage". Every January, Sheldon creates a vision board for what he wants to achieve in the new year. This year he wants to learn how to use chopsticks, to swim, to get his driver's license and, most importantly, he wants to write his first screenplay.

Sheldon, you are an absolute gift to all of us. Go out and continue your beautiful journey! ●

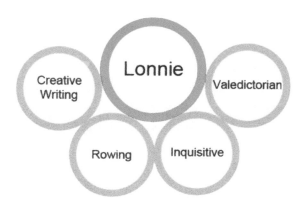

One day after school, I asked Lonnie if he would write his story for me. He hesitated before replying with a vague, "yes."

On October 12, 2021, my third period class started as it usually did, without a hitch. The announcements played in the background as I began to walk from my doorway to the front of the classroom. As I took my seat in front of all of the curious students, I called out, "Current events, does anyone have anything they want to discuss?" Several students raised their hands.

I called on each student one at a time. Each student demonstrated their aptitude in staying up to date with the current affairs as they brought up the different topics. Then, I called on another student who changed the course of class.

"Mr. Unger," the student said, "Yesterday, a student from Chaminade-Julienne died because he had a seizure while at rowing practice, and Chaminade canceled school today to mourn the student."

I was really saddened to hear about this particular event, and since I was curious about the details of such a tragedy, I pondered the situation openly with the class. "Yeah, I heard about that one. It's really an awful situation. I just wonder how that sort of thing happened. I wonder if they just could not stop his seizure. Just absolutely tragic."

One of my students stopped me as he interrupted my closing remarks. I was mid-thought, lingering on my last remark when he started to speak as tears formed in his eyes.

"He was on a boat in the river," Lonnie said, as he choked up with tears. "I was there." Lonnie began fully crying, cut off by his tears, and he became increasingly unable to speak as his lungs filled with his sniffling wallows. "He was on the river, in the back of the boat when he had the seizure. No one knew, those kids didn't know."

Lonnie found himself choked up as his tears streamed down his face. I called him up to me and asked him to take a moment in the hallway. I knew that he did not want to be crying in front of a full class of his senior peers, so I gave him the time he needed to calm down while he waited for five minutes in the hallway. I didn't know it at the time, but when he was out in the hallway, he was doing the same thing he had done every minute of every hour throughout that entire morning: he was reading an article about the boy's death. I could see that Lonnie was struggling to cope with the death of the boy, and I knew, just as he did, that his process of mourning, grieving, and sadness was far from over.

As he entered the classroom again, from the hallway, Lonnie grabbed a handful of tissues, and he resumed his seat with his head down, and his eyes red. I apologized to him as he settled back into his seat, and he accepted my apology with a quick reply. I could tell he no longer wanted to talk about the boy who had drowned, so I hastily continued our lessons for the class.

Lonnie

After class, I stopped Lonnie as he was leaving the room. I grabbed his shoulder, emphasizing my words, as I said to him, "Those kids on your team are gonna need you. You've got to be there for them. They're gonna look up to you because of your age. Be there for them." Lonnie agreed, knowing that what I said was entirely true. Again, I did not know it at the time, but what I had said, had really impacted Lonnie and his thoughts and his approach to whole mourning process. Lonnie was content to just let things pass by without ever mentioning a thing to anyone. He was ready to quit his team, and he was ready to just sit things out in silence. He did reveal to me later, however, that my emphasis on his age, and, more importantly, my emphasis on his need to guide those who were younger than him, encouraged him to do just that. He decided to attend a team counseling session on Friday of that week.

By no means did my advice end his grieving process. It took months of introspection on his part. However, he eventually revealed to me that what I had said, stuck with as a reminder of how things have to work in a world that keeps moving forward, regardless of personal sorrow—and that was how he ultimately made it through his grieving process.

So, when I asked him to write his story one fateful day after class, I did not know that I was asking Lonnie to produce his first successful attempt at writing about those events he had experienced on October 11, 2021. However, I came to my own realization, just like Lonnie, about what the story meant. In life, like in discussions that may have to start out innocently one day in a third period classroom, things happen fast, and unpredictably. There is no one way to determine how an event may unfold. There isn't any way of knowing if one's final moment may be his/her last one. You can't live your whole life envisioning that every subsequent event will be your last one or else you will feel exhausted waiting for a moment that may never come. What you can do, however, is to take a lesson from Joshua 1:9 in the Bible and remember a friend or a loved one through God and memories: "Life can be full of challenges, sorrows and tough decisions. But even amidst hardship, the Lord counsels us to be strong and courageous."

Lonnie and I have developed quite a teacher-student relationship. I want to thank Lonnie for sharing his very personal and introspective lesson. Lonnie, you have helped me deal with my own losses. To all those who are reading, don't ever forget:

"Courage is found in unlikely places."
Tolkien

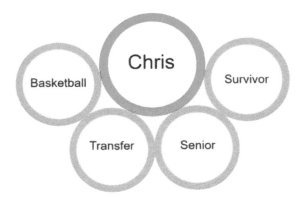

I recall a student in my class, a young man named Chris.

I am a man who likes to stick to his routine. Every day I come to school it's the same thing.

When I come in early, something that I always try to do, I review my lessons for the day. I look at the objective I'm trying to teach in my classes; I go over questions I want to ask each day to engage the students. I will also pull up some supplementary materials on the computer. I'll go to the library in the building for some extra research or materials on the topic for the day, or I'll even run into the copy room and print something off that I might need that day.

One morning I returned to my classroom after my usual routine, and a student, Chris, was sitting in my room. He was sitting in the front seat, first row, same place he's been all year. Now, I didn't mind him being there, but I found it a little peculiar since it was so early in the morning. It wasn't anything too concerning. Sometimes students like to stop in and say 'hello' every once in a while. Nothing wrong with that.

Chris was an 18-year-old African American student who had transferred from another school in the Dayton area. He was average in height and had an Afro. At the time I had taught six American History classes, and he happened to be in one of them. Normally, my classes were made up of exclusively freshmen, but he was a senior. Before he had transferred, he had never taken this particular class, and he needed it to graduate. He was a good sport about it, and I never had any problems with him. Chris had always sat in the front row, first seat, ready to learn whatever I was dishing out that day. He was a good student: quiet in class, raised his hand when he was supposed to and asked good questions. I always liked having a senior in an all freshman classes. I could tell he was a good kid, a smart kid. He had a good head on his shoulders, and I was excited to see where he would go in his life.

So, when I saw him, I said, "Hey, good morning Chris, what's going on? Why are you here so early?"

He replied without any hesitation, "Unger, can we talk?"

So I sat down, I put aside the papers that I had copied onto my desk and looked him right in the eye. I said, "Give it to me. What do you have?"

Chris said,

"Mr. Unger, last night I went to visit my grandma up in North Dayton. I parked the car in her driveway and went inside. I had a good time. It was a nice visit. She fixed me dinner, and we talked for the longest time about her life and how school was going for me and that kind of stuff. When it started to get late, I decided to head out. I kissed her goodbye and went out to my car. I started the engine, and then there was a gun to the back of my head. I froze. The guy told me he wanted my wallet."

I asked, "Did you give it to him, Chris?"

"I gave him my wallet, Mr. Unger. I tried to stay as still as possible, and I handed it to him from my back pocket. All the while, I could feel the cold metal of the gun pressed against the back of my head. I froze—I've never been so scared in my life."

"Then, that was the end of it," he continued. "He got out of the car and took off into the night. And all the while I just sat there for about twenty minutes, shaking. I froze."

I paused for a minute, then I asked, "Chris, why are you telling me all of this? Do you want me to call someone?"

"Mr. Unger, did I do the right thing?"

He looked at me with an expression I had never seen on him before. However, it was still very familiar. I had seen it a thousand times. It was the face of a man who had brushed elbows with death. Something that would stay with him for the rest of his life. What I said to him next, I wanted it to stick with him just as well,

"Chris, you're sitting here telling me this story. You absolutely did the right thing. If you had resisted, you might not be here right now. You did the right thing," I told him firmly "Were you afraid?"

Chris said, "I was petrified. I was shaking, Mr. Unger. I'm not a big guy. I'm only five foot seven inches. I mean, I'm on the basketball team, but, hey, that doesn't mean much. I'm not a big guy."

"So, you didn't think about resisting?"

"I thought about it for a quick second. It crossed my mind, but I couldn't. The gun was inches away from my head," he admitted.

"Promise me you'll always remember you're braver than you believe."
Christopher Robin

I was proud of him. I was proud of him for doing what he did, and I was proud of him for coming and telling me all of this. I told Chris to listen, because I wanted him to remember what I had to say next.

"Chris, if you had done something drastic and that person had pulled the trigger on you, then you would have been a statistic. You would not be on the basketball team today, wouldn't be the A student that you are, you wouldn't be in the National Honors Society and you wouldn't graduate in May.

Because of what you did, you're going to do all of those things, and people are going to remember you for all those things and not some unlucky kid who got shot."

"But Mr. Unger," he started, "I think I don't feel right about this. I feel like I could have done more. Did I punk myself out? Do you really think I did the right thing?"

I'll say it again, Chris. **"You did exactly the right thing. You did everything right. You have so much to offer this world. If you weren't here, we'd all be cheated."**

He just sat there with this stunned expression on his face. He was a good kid... is a good kid. I don't want him to be remembered for something as stupid as that. He had to move on with his life. Nowadays, he's a practicing attorney, and a damn good one, at that.

Chris said, "Damn, Unger, I needed that."

"Chris, I'm glad we had this chat. Now you have to do one favor for me. When you go home tonight, I want you to sit down with your dad. Have you talked to you dad about all of this?"

"No, Unger, I have not talked to my dad."

"I want you to talk to your dad. I want you to tell him exactly what you told me right now, and listen to what he has to say, get a feel for what your dad is saying. Then, I want you to come in tomorrow and see me again. I want to talk to you again and see how you feel."

He told me he would, then he got up to leave for his first class. As he was leaving, the last thing I said to him was, "You know Chris, you coming in this morning and telling me this, telling me what happened—I'm honored. I feel honored that you sat across from me and told me this story. I hope you have a good rest of your day."

I think that as a teacher, one of the jobs we all have is to provide a platform to students so that they can talk to us. I think that words are powerful, and that language shapes how we think. I think that if we create a space for students to talk and listen effectively, they'll become more well-rounded people. It can help them grow as individuals and feel that they not only have a voice, but an important voice. Some teachers don't encourage that kind of thing, but I think as teachers, we need to provide a platform where students can engage us, and we can encourage this by asking the right questions. We can help provide this platform, and with that responsibility comes the fact that we have to invite dissenting opinions and help cultivate and accept those opinions. We have to encourage them to think on their own and share what they believe. When they share, they build connections. That day Chris and I shared a connection. Talking and connecting the way Chris and I did that day, helps with the process. It helps a teacher figure out how to deal with things that kids may not be entirely equipped to deal with on their own. It helps with the process and learning. Chris and I had a connection that was very special and I'm so very glad he's with us. ●

Social and Political Activism

Maurice • Jared • Coco • Adam H. • Neko • Maggie • Lucas

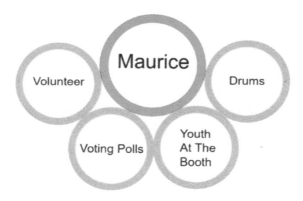

Maurice asked me, "Unger, can I work the voting polls on Election Day this year?" The Montgomery County Board of Elections sponsors "Youth at the Booth." It is a program for those who are 17 and 18 years old or a high school senior. They are able to serve as poll workers in Ohio. The Ohio Secretary of State asks teachers to identify those eligible high school seniors who wish to be part of the democratic process. Since poll workers are essential to running elections, Ohio's 88 county election boards rely on over 3500 patriotic Ohioans to operate the voting locations and assist fellow voters with casting their ballot.

Students earn $150 for their time, but they must attend a three-hour workshop that informs and educates them on working the polls. On Election Day, students must report half an hour before the polls open, remain all day and close up after the polls. Those students who are 18 can also vote during their break. Participating students receive community service hours, receive credit from their school and may report their service on their college applications. This program proves that young adult can actively control, contribute and make a difference in the election process.

When I introduce the program, we discuss voting participation and the registration process that is used by different states. With the rise of social media and the increase of political awareness in young people, more students are becoming politically active, and they want to make a difference in the political process. I have been working with Robyn Peke at the Montgomery County Board of Elections for ten years. Each fall, our high school will have from 75-85 seniors who work the polls on Election Day.

After Election Day, my classroom has discussions for half of the class period on how the day at the polls went for those students who had volunteered. One student said, "Mr. Unger, a woman who looked like she was in her 60s came in and voted for the first time ever." When Barack Obama was running, one of the students said, "I want to vote for Barack Obama, that's all I wanna do. Show me how to vote for him." Another student talked about the necessity of having patience with some voters who are rude. For example, in the precinct where this student was working, there were many white people voting. The student who made the comment about the rudeness, was African American, and a number of the white people asked the student what was the reason for working at the polls. Other students mentioned that some of the poll workers were interested in the name of their school and why they had been interested in becoming involved in the voting program. Several students helped assist handicapped people. Most of the experiences that my students shared were positive.

Maurice filled out all of the paperwork. He had to complete an application and a registration, but he had a problem with transportation to the polling area. I volunteered to take him to the precinct where he was to work. I picked up Maurice around 5:45 A.M. and bought him breakfast on the way to his precinct. I introduced him to his Precinct Captain because I wanted to make sure he was as comfortable as he could be, as he would be there for the whole day.

When I picked up Maurice at 7:30 that evening, I asked, **"Did you have a good day?"**

"Mr. Unger, I didn't realize how really important today was. Voting is important. It's a privilege and a right that all adults in America have. We have so many problems, and voting is how we can solve local, state and national issues," he explained. **"I haven't always been politically active, but your class has made me that way. So, I am so glad you motivated me to better understand our democratic process. By the way, when am I going to get paid?"** Maurice and I shared a laugh.

> **"Voting is the expression of our commitment to ourselves, one another, this country, and this world."**
> *Sharon Salzberg*

"It'll be about a week-and-a-half until they can process it, and then you'll get a check in the mail, If you don't receive it, come to me and we'll talk to them about that," I explained.

"Youth in the Booth" is a win-win project. The community benefits as well as the student participants. Over the 10 years that I have worked with this program, I have placed over 750 students in it. This means that the students have been able to earn $113,000, and they have also learned that voting is a citizen opportunity to have their opinion heard. I remember Maurice telling me that voting in our elections was not a spectator sport, that all of us have to participate actively. He also shared with me that he couldn't wait until he was 18 so that he could vote in the next election. I hope that Maurice doesn't forget his privilege, because there are segments of our society that would very much like us to *not* vote, or for our vote to *not* count. ●

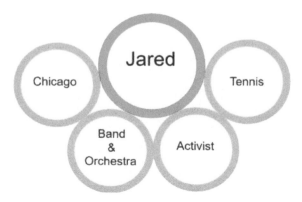

Jared showed up at my door during the last period of a school day during the month of May. It was totally unexpected. He had graduated from Stivers School for the Arts the year before and had just finished his freshman year at Xavier University. Jared had been an excellent student in high school, making all A's in mainly AP classes of Calculus, Literature, Composition and Biology. His art magnet had been band and orchestra—he was a talented musician. He had also been a tennis athlete.

I had had Jared for two of my classes, Sociology and Government. He had always been an immensely well-spoken young man, although before he spoke, while he thinking about his choice of words, he had a habit of being unable to establish eye contact.

In my Sociology class, we had explored a unit on the ethnicities that comprise the United States. One of those units included indigenous peoples within our country. We explored religions, tribes and their unique regions, but most importantly, we had discussed the Trail of Tears. All of my students knew about the Cherokee Trail of Tears, but I always tried to inform them that every tribe had their own trail of tears that would lead to their reservation. We discussed reservation life and the genocide of Native Americans in our country. At the end of this unit, my students had to pick a tribe and write an informational paper that explored the region of the tribe, its leaders and their cultural characteristics. Once their papers were finished, each student would present their findings to the class. Jared had done a fine job with the Lakota Tribe.

After our initial handshake, I introduced Jared to the class telling them that he was a student at Xavier and telling them that he had received a number of scholarships from different universities, but that he had chosen Xavier because they had a great business school and had provided him with a full ride. He shared some of his experiences from his freshman year, while I reminisced about the type of student he had been during his time at Stivers. I shared my knowledge of Jared's academic achievements, his musical talents and the great ability he had to engage others in conversation. Of course, I had to mention that he had also been on the tennis team.

Before Jared had chosen Xavier, we had talked,

"You know you're going to be a minority there, Jared. There aren't many African American men and women at Xavier. Just make sure you're ready for that."

Jared had replied, "Unger, I'm okay with that."

I asked him a question after I had introduced him to the class.

"So, was Xavier an easy fit?"

"No, it really wasn't," Jared answered, "I had to get involved in a variety of clubs, and I played intramural tennis, but I did eventually make a fit."

I followed up with another question, trying to pull more information from him.

"So, tell me more about your year, what are some of the highlights?"

He informed the class of some of the highlights and then answered some student questions.

"Did you do a spring break?" I interjected. "Isn't that what college guys do, go on a spring break?"

Jared hesitated for a quick second or two then gave me a soft laugh and said,

"No, I didn't go on a traditional spring break. I went on an alternative spring break."

"Woah! I've heard about those." I continued with another question. "So, an alternative spring break; exactly what is an alternative spring break?"

Jared went on to tell of the experience. "Well, that's when a group of students at a university get together, and they either go abroad to a different country, or they stay within the states, with the objective of fostering dialogue and making relationships with a host community around issues of social justice. By working alongside the people and sharing stories, we learn more about ourselves and the world."

"So, you've become kind of a change agent?"

Jared answered confidently, "Yes, I have acknowledged and become more aware of the things that are happening in the places around me."

"Fantastic," I said. "So, tell me more about this spring break."

"Well, it was myself and a vanload of about 10 students, and we went to the Pine Ridge Reservation in South Dakota. This is the Oglala Lakota Indian Reservation. We teamed up with three other vans, one from Arizona, one from Penn State and one from Michigan. Altogether, there were about 40 of us."

"So, what did you do there?"

"We insulated and sided houses with vinyl, built bunk beds, repaired leaks and installed protective skirting along mobile homes to keep heat in and water out."

"Did you stay there?"

"Yes, we lived right on the reservation, eating the food they provided, and immersing ourselves in their culture. The whole thing lasted for about eight days."

"Bet you were exhausted."

"Oh yeah, I volunteered eight to ten hours a day," he admitted.

"So, what did you think?" I asked.

Jared concluded, "It was one of the greatest experiences of my life."

I began to puzzle. "Why'd you do it?"

"Well, in your class, when you taught that unit on Native Americans, you put out there all the different stuff about Native Americans, and I wanted to see if you were right. I wanted to see it for myself?"

I questioned, "And did you?"

"Everything we discussed in class was evident," he said. "It's all there, the overall percent living below the poverty line. It's all there. Not having enough housing, being overcrowded, it's there. Not having enough medical help, it's there. Everything we discussed and wrote about, was there."

"What about the others who went there with you to help?" I asked. "What were they like?"

"They were all college students, mostly middle to upper class, mostly Caucasian and mostly female. But they were all activists, and I really liked that."

After he explained a little bit more and the class asked him more questions, our conversation had pretty much ended. A goodbye and a hug was shared, then he was gone. We decided that year to keep in touch through text.

The following year, Jared showed up at my door again. He had finished his sophomore year. He asked if he could talk about his second alternative spring break.

"Where did you go this time," I asked curiously. "Albany, New York, and we did work with gangs and the alternative choices that kids can have in school."

We had another repeat performance from Jared at the end of his third year, when he returned again.

"Another alternative spring break," I predicted.

"Yeah, I worked in New York with homeless people, kids and other people on the street," he replied. "It was great, another eye opener."

I wasn't surprised when Jared appeared again, at the end of his senior year. "Alternative spring break again?"

"Yeah, but this time I wanted to treat myself. I went to Jamaica. We dug wells and retrieved clean water, but I did hang out on the beach and drink a little rum sometimes."

I chuckled, enjoying this news from him. "So, you finally got to the beach and treated yourself after four years of alternative spring breaks? Fantastic!"

> **"I'm guided by what I'm really outraged about and what I think I can actually try to influence. And it may be that I can only influence things one case at a time, but ultimately, the plan is always to try and improve the system."**
> *Amal Clooney*

When you do these alternative spring breaks, the purpose of them is to travel the United States or abroad to help others and gain information about the world, but in doing so you also end up gaining information about yourself.

I have always been an advocate for student activism. I've always tried to promote political, environmental, economic and social change. I believe that student activism has especially surged in the past two decades with young people calling on leaders to ease inequality and to secure a better future. But, it's nothing new. In the '60s and early '70s we had the anti-Vietnam war movement and the Civil Rights movements and most of these activities were propelled by high school and college students.

Currently students are really into the "me too" movement. We have the "Black Lives Matter" movement. We have the LGBTQ+ movement. We have gun violence issues. We have climate change. We have voter registration, and much more. Today's young people can expand. There are many different movements if a student is interested in becoming active. They also have a tool that I was never able to use and that is the web and social media.

If young people really want to be activists, they have to be educated on the purpose of the cause. They can't do it just because other people are doing it, and they have to be able to take action. I have a quote in my room and it says, "Once there is seeing, there must be acting, otherwise whats the point in seeing." It's a Vietnamese Buddhist quote.

Finally, I think if a young person wants to be an activist, they must be open to discussion and dialogue with others. They've GOT to do that. I think if we compare the '60s, involvement today is similar to that of 50 years ago. Our nation was divided in many ways as it is today, and many young people are dedicating themselves to projects that CAN make a difference.

Last summer I ran into Jared while I was visiting my daughter, Emily, in Chicago. I was sitting on a bench in front of a little hotel in the Lincoln Park area waiting for my daughter so we could go out for lunch. As I sat there reading the newspaper, I noticed somebody walk by and then stop right in front of me. With the newspaper in my face, I looked down and saw the toes of some shoes pointing toward me. I put the paper down, revealing...Jared.

"Unger, is that you?"

"Yeah, Jared, it's me. How are you doing?"

He looked down at me and said, "Well, I'm doing great! How odd is it running into you in Chicago on a Sunday morning."

I called my daughter, and it turned out she was busy, so Jared and I went out to lunch. Jared is currently working in the financial district in Chicago, and he also tutors kids on weekends through a school program.

"By the way, I wanted to thank you for the donations you made to our alternative spring break program," Jared said warmly.

"What are you talking about?" I wanted to know.

"Well, I know that my university sent out letters, requesting donations."

"Yeah, I did send something back," I exclaimed, "but I told them I wanted to remain anonymous."

"They told me that it was from a teacher from my high school, so I knew it was you." Jared gave me a friendly smile, which in turn made me smile as well.

Jared, be a change agent—I am proud of you!

"The greatness of a community is most accurately measured by the compassionate actions of its members."
Coretta Scott King

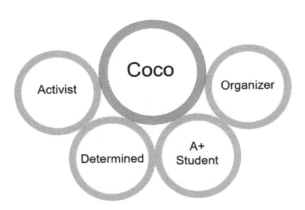

"Why can't we get Ambassador Tony Hall to come to Stivers, Mr. Unger?" asked Coco. "We should be able to do something like that!"

Ever since 2015, I have had everyone in my Senior Government Class write a 1,000-word essay about the professional life and successes of Ambassador Tony Hall. They had to meet the requirements set by the John F. Kennedy (JFK) library and then I would submit some of the essays to the Profile in Courage Award every year. The essay is part of our study of the Legislative Branch. This is a private award given to recognize those who display an immense courage similar to those illustrated in the book by JFK of the same name. It is given to individuals who are still alive and who are either elected officials or were elected previously. These individuals, through their actions in accord with their conscience, must have risked their careers or lives to pursue a bigger vision of national, international, state or local interest in opposition to their constituents' personal interests. The winners of the award are selected by a committee, which is named by the John F. Kennedy Library Foundation, which usually includes members of the JFK family. The award is usually presented by John F. Kennedy's daughter, Caroline. The winner is awarded a sterling silver lantern which is patterned after the lantern depicted on the U.S. Constitution.

Last year, 2022, Mitt Romney received the award for his consistent and courageous defense of democracy, as well as his vote to impeach Donald Trump. He as the first senator to vote against a president of his own party. Other recipients of the award have included John Lewis for his leadership in the Civil Rights Movements, Alberto J. Mora for his conviction of the illegal tactics used at Guantanamo Bay, Elizabeth Redenbaugh for standing up against segregation in the United States and Nancy Pelosi for expanding health care and for her creation of the most diverse Congress in U.S. history in its time. The award was created in 1989, and it is always presented each May.

The contest is open for ninth through twelfth graders who are homeschooled or for those who attend parochial, private or public schools. Participants must write an essay that explains why they have chosen their candidate and why this person deserves to receive the next award for the Profile in Courage. Previous recipients are no longer eligible unless it is for a different act of courage. Essay submissions are judged on content and presentation, with 500-1,000 words, with a minimum of five sources. All essays must be original. The winning essay receives a $10,000 award, second place receives $3,000, and five other finalists receive $1,000. Each semi-finalist receives $100 and ten students receive honorable mentions. All participating students receive a certificate of participation.

Ambassador Tony Hall donated all of his professional papers to the Wright State University Library. I initially went there three years ago to pour over his papers to see if they would meet the JFK Library requirements for the Profile in Courage Award. I spent three weeks going through countless boxes of the Ambassador's papers, including letters that he wrote and received, awards, hate mail and a variety of other documents. When I finished, I concluded that Ambassador Hall's work over the past four decades has *absolutely* been a gift to America.

Once I had confirmed my beliefs, I took about 15 students after school to Wright State's archives. We continued to return to the library until the students could gather enough information that would be relevant to their essays. After all of us had verbally evaluated what we believed was the most worthwhile, I collected all of it and then put the information in folders for each of the senior students. We decided that we needed an outline from the Ambassador's material on the Select Committees on Hunger. The next discussion involved diamond mining and at what cost is diamond mining. Hall had written a bill about conflict diamonds or blood diamonds. Additionally, we discussed Hall's apology for slavery, and followed up that with his *Conscience Clause* and his work on issues of abortion within the Democratic Party. The outline was finalized with a look at this book, *The Changing Face of Hunger.* I included some excerpts from this book with the other info in the folders. Part of our ongoing effort to consider Hall had us looking at videos where he had been a participant. The best video out there is *Ted Talk* where he summarizes his work on hunger in Africa and his relationship with Mother Theresa.

Each student was required to complete an essay outline which would help them gather their materials, as well as their thoughts in writing a cohesive essay. Their claim in the essay would read something like: "Ambassador Tony Hall risked his career and life to take stands based on the dictates of good rather than the dictates of the poll, interest groups

Coco

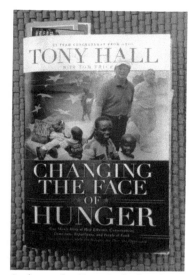

Ambassador Tony Hall's book

and even constituents." The students would then complete the three points of evidence. Before their actual writing began, the students came together in groups to compare and contrast their outlines.

> "You know, Coco, I've never actually thought about having Ambassador Tony Hall at our school. I'm not sure what that would take...I know he's a *very very* busy man in Washington D.C., and he travels *all* over the world. He's currently work-ing with a program called *Alliance to End Hunger,* and I don't even know if we can get him here. I do know that he has an organization here in Dayton called the *Hall Hunger Initiative*."

I could tell by Coco's eyes that she would have none of this; so I put Coco in charge.

> "I'll put this in your hands then, Coco. If there is a way to figure this out, let's see what we can do. Tell you what, I know inside the boxes of information on Ambassador Hall, his agent is identified. I will get that number, pass it on to you and we will see what we can do."

When I found the number of the agent, I contacted him to let him know that we were interested in talking to Tony Hall. I put him in touch with Coco, and they began coordinating.

A day or two later, while I was staying late after school, as I do sometimes to grade papers, I heard my phone ring. Since I was grading papers, I didn't answer the phone, but it kept ringing. Finally, I picked it up, and to my surprise, it was none other than Ambassador Tony Hall on the line.

"Mr. Unger, my agent, said that you and another student were trying to arrange a meeting where we could get together. Maybe we could do a Skype. I'm going to tell my agent and he will talk to Coco. We will see what we can do to meet through a virtual meeting?"

"The great responsibility I feel is to get people to put power and hope in themselves."
Amanda Gorman

Coco and I found a date that worked for Ambassador Hall, as well as my seniors, and the meeting was set. I readied my students to have a few questions they could ask the Ambassador during the meeting. After I had looked through the questions to see which ones could give them the most information for their paper, we were ready to go.

After this preparation, all of us met in the auditorium during the last period of the day. Sure enough, after counting down the seconds to the call, Ambassador Hall was on the screen. We had a microphone set up in front so the students could ask their questions. I spent 10-15 seconds to introduce the Ambassador because I knew that he was so humble that he would *not* want to talk about himself. He just is not that kind of person. After he said a few words himself, Ambassador Tony Hall opened up the floor for the seniors of Stivers to ask him questions. For the next 50 minutes, the back and forth between the ambassador and the students was unforgettable. All of the students who were in attendance took notes so they could use his quotes or thoughts in their essays.

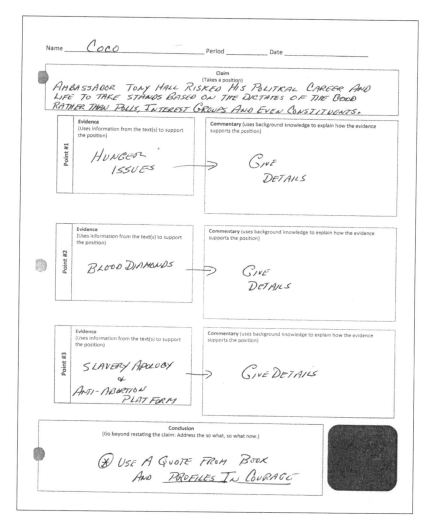

Name _____*Coco*_____ Period _____ Date _____

Claim
(Takes a position)
AMBASSADOR TONY HALL RISKED HIS POLITKAL CAREER AND LIFE TO TAKE STANDS BASED ON THE DICTATES OF THE GOOD RATHER THAN POLLS, INTEREST GROUPS AND EVEN CONSTITUENTS.

Point #1

Evidence
(Uses information from the text(s) to support the position)

HUNGER ISSUES →

Commentary (uses background knowledge to explain how the evidence supports the position)

GIVE DETAILS

Point #2

Evidence
(Uses information from the text(s) to support the position)

BLOOD DIAMONDS →

Commentary (uses background knowledge to explain how the evidence supports the position)

GIVE DETAILS

Point #3

Evidence
(Uses information from the text(s) to support the position)

SLAVERY APOLOGY & ANTI-ABORTION PLATFORM →

Commentary (uses background knowledge to explain how the evidence supports the position)

GIVE DETAILS

Conclusion
(Go beyond restating the claim: Address the so what, so what now.)

(*) USE A QUOTE FROM BOOK AND *PROFILES IN COURAGE*

It was a resounding success!

When it was all over, and after the students had left, I went back up to my classroom to grade some more papers. I thought to myself, how lucky we all had been to have made this happen. While I was sitting there, my phone rang. Although I thought it strange that someone was calling my room after school, I answered the phone to hear Ambassador Tony Hall on the other line again.

"Mr. Unger, I was just having dinner with my wife, and I'm sharing with her what a great experience I had with your class today. Thank you so much for giving me the opportunity to talk and to share with young people. However, I have one request for you. When the students compose their essays, could you send me some of those papers? I would love to see how they put it all together."

"Absolutely!" I said.

I had my students write their papers, and my colleagues evaluated them. I submitted about a dozen of them to the John F. Kennedy Library for the competition. Carolyn T., Isabelle K., and Kayla C. all received Honorable Mentions for their eloquent writing. I do have to say that I was a little bit disappointed, not in the students, but because I was *positive* that the story of Ambassador Hall would merit the award, and the way the students put their work together made me believe that winning would be a great possibility.

The next day I had to speak to Coco.

"Coco, your tenacity and determination made Ambassador Hall's appearance happen. You got him here! You arranged the screen setup, you set up the sound system, and you did the camera work. You really pulled it off! You were incredible in helping me achieve the goal of bringing Ambassador Hall's legacy to life to re-establish his relevance and to amplify his call to service. You should be *so* proud. I am so proud of you."

"Young and full of spirit is not a bad thing."
MLK

Coco went to Antioch College in Yellow Springs after her graduation from high school, and she is still doing great things. Later that summer, I met in person with Ambassador Hall when he came to Dayton to be a featured speaker at a dinner honoring all the Peace Corps volunteers from Dayton. He asked about the Stivers students and said, "I'd like to come back one day and address your senior class. Maybe we can arrange that in the future."

The overall experience of having done research at the library over a period of weeks, the students who had done the research, all of the students' writing papers, Coco's arrangement to meet Ambassador Tony Hall over Skype and the relationship that Stivers now has with Ambassador Hall, will resonate with me as one of the highlights of my 50 years of teaching. •

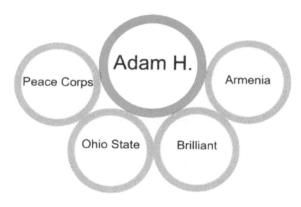

"Adam," I said, "You've got so much promise. You've got so much going on, you've gotta get it together. You've got so many talents. You can be a changemaker. You've got to try to do more."

Adam sat in the back of my freshman American History class. He seemed to pay attention, and he was never absent however he never turned in an assignment. He just didn't do anything.

His lack of performance was the same each quarter. I tried everything I could to figure out if something was wrong. I would call his mother, and I tried to talk to his older sister who was in one of my other classes, but nothing really worked. Adam ended up failing my class for both semesters. He had to take credit recovery for American History.

However, at that time he didn't know that I also taught Senior Government. That meant three years later he'd be walking into my classroom again. His behavior was still the same, non confrontational and quiet, but he still didn't do his assignments. Again, I spoke with his mother regularly, but there were still no changes. Even a couple of home visits made no difference. I decided that something drastic had to happen.

When the second quarter started, at the end of the first day of class while the students were filing out of the room with Adam bringing up the rear, right before he reached the door, I walked over and locked it. Now it was just him and me. He looked at me with a puzzled expression. I leaned in as close as I could, perhaps three inches away, and then I lost my temper.

"Adam, it's the middle of the year and you haven't done a damn thing! When are you gonna wake the hell up? We went through the same thing over three years ago, and you still haven't a clue. You have so much talent You actually could become a changemaker if you actually put in the work. You've got me at my wits' end. You have to wake up here and get it together. You gotta start doing something. I don't know what to say to you, but sooner or later that light in you has to go on. Why are you wasting everyone's time?"

It was then that I realized I had been yelling at him the whole time. I wish I had chosen my words a little more carefully, but I had said all I had to say. After I had given him my 'two cents,' he didn't say a word. I moved out of his way and he left.

When Adam came back the following week, he was a changed young man. He never missed an assignment, and everything was turned in on time. Adam had gone from a 'zero' his first quarter to one hundred percent the second quarter. He aced the exam for the semester and, was by all accounts, an outstanding student.

When the second semester began, he knocked it out of the park again. Although he didn't raise his hand or get involved in classroom discussions, I could tell from his writing and the assignments that he knew everything that had been discussed. Adam knew what he was doing, and his work showed that perfectly.

When he graduated from Stivers, Adam was unable to go to a conventional college because of his GPA. His test scores were high, but his overall grades were greatly impacted by his earlier apathy. With that in mind, Adam decided to enroll at the local community college, Sinclair. He took his general education classes for a year and then he transferred to Ohio State where he majored in political science and had produced outstanding work in all of his classes. He graduated "cum laude", with high honors.

While he attended Ohio State, he took a fair share of Russian classes. When he finished his undergraduate work, he left the United States and continued his studies in Siberia. Ultimately, he returned to the United States and applied for the Peace Corps.

Peace Corps emblem

The Peace Corps is an independent governmental agency and a volunteer program run by the U.S. government, providing international social and economic development. Volunteers are American citizens, typically with a college degree or some type of useful skill. Once in the Peace Corps, the volunteers normally work overseas for a period of two years. More than 249,000 Americans have joined the Peace Corps in over 142 countries. At the end of the two-year stint, a volunteer can request to stay an extra year. During the application process, your skill levels are examined in six project areas: agriculture, environment, health, education, youth or youth development and community or economic development. Adam went through the arduous interviewing process and was accepted, aided by the fact that he had lived abroad already.

Adam was selected to live in Armenia, an eastern European country, teaching English in schools. From what I've heard, the school he taught in was a pretty tough environment. There was less than an average amount of electricity, and when winters would become freezing cold, Adam was moved to organize projects that would raise money to create a better working school environment.

"If you are an activist you are not entitled to lose hope."
Nathan Law

Two years had passed, and I was still teaching at Stivers. One day after classes had let out, I heard a knock at the door and there was Adam. I invited him in while we exchanged pleasantries.

"Do you remember me, Mr. Unger? My name is Adam and—"
I laughed and said, "Yeah, of course, I remember you."

He gave a nervous chuckle. "I didn't know if you remembered me...or if you even wanted to remember me."

"Adam, I never want to forget you. You were an exceptional student. I've been keeping up with you, and I know you've been in the Peace Corp."

"Hey, Unger, can I talk to the class tomorrow? I have a presentation I'd like to show them."

On the following day he came in with a PowerPoint presentation with dozens of photographs of what he did in Armenia. After it was over I asked him,

"Do you think you're gonna go back?

"Mr. Unger, I wanna go back," he said excitedly. "I, gonna ask for an extension for one more year. I love it there so much, and the kids are so great. I actually have an idea I'd like to run by you. When I go back, can I Skype with you and your class once a month? I'd like my class to get together with yours so they can watch how you teach, and your class could watch how I teach. I'd really like it if we could have the students interact. I think it could be enriching for them."

"Absolutely," I said. I couldn't wait to get started.

We committed to that for all of the following year. Once a month we would start a call, and the kids loved it. It was a great success.

Adam returned from the Peace Corps.

Adam returned to the United States after his extra year, and he enrolled at the University of Maine to get his masters degree in "Peace Building in Conflict Transformation." Today, he is currently working on his doctorate and is recognized as a Senior Peace Corp Recruiter.

The next time I saw him, he told me about all of the people he's gotten interested in joining the Peace Corp. I asked him how he felt about what he was doing.

"Unger, I've helped people," he said. "I think I've had a huge impact I think I made somebody's life better."

"You've done so much more than that Adam. You've made a difference. You are the changemaker I always thought you could be."

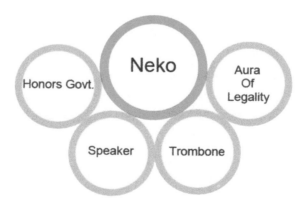

As I was leaving the graduation at the Masonic Temple, I was absolutely awestruck by the lesson I had just learned from the student I had been teaching for the past year. Neko caught up to me and reaffirmed his message in just a few words, "Unger, I remember everything you have ever said."

I do not teach AP Government, I teach Honors Government. Years ago, the principal came to me and asked me to teach the seniors AP Government, and I told her simply and respectfully that I did not want to teach AP. Teaching any AP requires that, above all else, a teacher focuses exclusively on teaching students about the AP test. If I'm charged with teaching government to the best and the brightest of the seniors who would come to take AP Government, I want to focus on more than just a test. As opposed to an AP Government course, the principal and I negotiated a concession. I would teach seniors who wanted to take the AP test in an Honors Government class, but I would not teach strictly to the test. My philosophy was, and still is, that if I am teaching students at an honors pace with the merit of an honors class, then they will always be ready for the AP test. Let me be the first to say that the students always rise to the occasion.

Those students who take my honors class are special. While the students in my honors classes may always vary by their race, religion, cultural ethnic backgrounds, and especially their political opinions, it seems that one thing is always a constant in my honors classes: the students have a love for learning and a desire to immerse themselves in the material.

When Neko first entered my class in September, I could see that he was quiet, the type of student that didn't care to talk. At times it seemed that he was barely paying attention. I knew that Neko had signed up for my honors class, but for some reason, he was not responsive. However, I always had an underlying suspicion that when he finally did talk, we would all be surprised. I did know that Neko was in the National Honors Society and that he was a terrific trombone player. Other than this, I knew little about the exceptional young man who sat so quietly in my room.

As the year moved forward, Neko provided little conversation, but he worked hard on each assignment as we moved through the many units of American government. We covered the Constitution in detail, and subsequently the Legislative Branch and the Executive Branch. The area of government that we covered most was last, the Judicial Branch. Every year when I finally get to the Judicial Branch, I start off by showing a film in my class called, *Disturbing the Universe*, a documentary, based on the accounts of William Kunstler's daughters. The film focuses on the life of the infamous lawyer, William Kunstler, following World War II. The documentary covers the varying types of cases that William Kunstler represented, ranging from civil rights cases in the South with the ACLU and key figures like Martin Luther King Jr., to the Wounded Knee Occupation in 1973. A more notorious case was Kunstler's defense of Yousef Salaam (15 years old), part of the Central Park Five who was wrongly accused of the rape of a woman in Central Park in 1989. Essentially, Kunstler represented the cases of people and groups that other lawyers would not represent because of the negative publicity that would result from the cases. Kunstler provides young people with a positive example of challenging the powers of the status quo, motivated by public pressure and legally 'disturbing the universe'.

The film is always a hit in my government classes because it stimulates discussions that involve the whole class. Each time I show the documentary, students always ask why they've never heard about cases such as Attica or the Chicago 7. I always make it clear to them that regular history classes simply do not cover some of the more important and controversial parts of history. I make sure that students always leave my class educated on important matters including those of William Kunstler. My students write a reflective essay following this unit.

Neko

Stivers School for the Arts requires 5-C essays as a formula to

81

condense the fundamental characteristics of an essay into a short and sweet five-word acronym: claim, claim evidence, commentary, conclusion, and connection. It is a template-based writing that helps reaffirm the meaning of specific lessons. This is the format that they use when analyzing Kunstler, and it is a format that Stivers' students including those in my government class (including Neko) use numerous times throughout their Stivers' career. Because of the value of Kunstler socially, when they used this 5-C formula to demonstrate what they had learned, their essays turned out great! Neko and his class fully delivered on this assignment, and I admired the hell out of the way the students put so much effort into writing about not just the cases we discussed in class but even some that I had never heard about. One student wrote about a Kunstler case that set a precedent in the academic world. Because of this case, students are no longer able to be 'tracked' in their academics and later forced into studying specific subjects because of the previous tracking. I had never heard about this Kunstler case! I couldn't help but feel that Neko, however, was missing out on certain things in class. Although Neko wrote an admirable essay, and because I could tell he had been listening, I still felt that he was missing *something*.

As the year rapidly inched forward, Neko and the rest of his class continued to do well. The time seemed to come around too quickly for the senior class that I had come to admire so greatly to graduate. I always attend the graduation of the seniors, and it is for that reason that I know there are more speeches to be given by students than those of the Valedictorian and Salutatorian. However, in this particular year, I did not know who those additional students would be. Neko, of all people, went up to the stage, looking like a million bucks, ready to deliver some gold. I was unimaginably surprised!

The precipice of Neko's great speech was founded upon that faithful essay that I had once had Neko and his class write about, William Kunstler. Neko read from his essay, and he beautifully discussed Kunstler's philosophy. He took Kunstler's infatuation with Michelangelo's *David* and used the story of David versus Goliath, to relay the central premise of his speech, which was "Do I Dare?" Neko

William Kunstler by Julienne M.   Statue of David with Kunstler.

was amazing on that stage, and I could not help but feel a sense of relief when I realized that all the time I had worried about Neko, he had been learning. He had always worked to understand what he had been taught.

As Neko continued his speech, he captivated all of the audience, including me, as he ended his speech with the following quote from William Kunstler's *"Aura of Organized Society"*:

> *And that is the terrible myth of organized society, that everything that's done through the established system is legal—and that word has a powerful psychological impact. It makes people believe that there is an order to life, and an order to a system, and that a person that goes through this order and is convicted, has gotten all that is due to him. And therefore, society can turn its conscience off, and look to other things and other times.*
>
> *And that's the terrible thing about these past trials, is that they have this aura of legitimacy; this aura of legality. I suspect that better men than the world has known and more of them, have gone to their deaths through a legal system than through all the illegalities in the history of man.*
>
> *Six million people in Europe during the Third Reich? Legal*

Sacco Vanzetti? Quite legal.

The Haymarket defendants? Legal.

The hundreds of rape trials throughout the South where black men were condemned to death? All legal.

Jesus? Legal.

Socrates? Legal.

And that is the kaleidoscopic nature of what we live through here and in other places. Because all tyrants learn that it is far better to do this thing through some semblance of legality than to do it without that pretense.

You could have heard a pin drop in the Masonic Temple as Neko finished.

Neko absolutely 'nailed it' on that stage. He delivered the best graduation speech that I have ever heard. Prior to that moment, I barely knew whether that young man, up on the stage, had ever heard a word that I had said in class, let alone whether he was capable of applying it to the world. I was so impressed by his skills. I was so grateful to have had such an impressive man in my class.

As I was slipping out, trying to beat the crowd as I always do at senior graduations, Neko came running out of the auditorium doors as I was climbing into my car. As he stumbled to my car door he said, "Mr. Unger, Mr. Unger, I need to say something to you before you leave."

When Neko got to my car, he kept it short, just as he always had, and he said,

"I never said anything in class, and I never said anything the entire time, but I paid attention to everything in class. That Kunstler video stuck with me, and I'm going to dedicate my life to questioning and changing our institutions, and our systems."

He briefly paused to make sure that I was understanding his words, and he soon continued,

"Mr. Unger, you taught me that people have power, but you

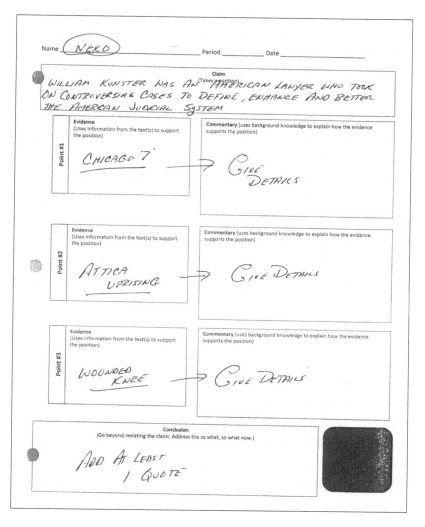

Name NEKO   Period   Date

Claim (Takes a position)
WILLIAM KUNSTER WAS AN AMERICAN LAWYER WHO TOOK ON CONTROVERSIAL CASES TO DEFINE, ENHANCE AND BETTER THE AMERICAN JUDICIAL SYSTEM

Point #1
Evidence (Uses information from the text(s) to support the position)
CHICAGO 7

Commentary (uses background knowledge to explain how the evidence supports the position)
GIVE DETAILS

Point #2
Evidence (Uses information from the text(s) to support the position)
ATTICA UPRISING

Commentary (uses background knowledge to explain how the evidence supports the position)
GIVE DETAILS

Point #3
Evidence (Uses information from the text(s) to support the position)
WOUNDED KNEE

Commentary (uses background knowledge to explain how the evidence supports the position)
GIVE DETAILS

Conclusion (Go beyond restating the claim: Address the so what, so what now.)
ADD AT LEAST 1 QUOTE

also taught me that we have to exert it, and that those people in power have to answer to us. That is what I learned from you."

Neko and I exchanged hugs and said our final farewells. Before I drove away and ended that school year, I called to Neko who was walking away, and I had to tell him, with one final commendation, "Neko, you're the best and the brightest, and I am so proud that you took a lesson that I put together, and made it yours. I hope that you always dare."

There's a quote that I remember from time to time when I get to thinking about Neko. The quote originates from Margaret Mead, and I think it sums up Neko and his undeniable legacy in the best way that words can.

"Never doubt that a small group of thoughtful, committed citizens can change the world. Indeed, it is the only thing that ever has."

When faced with critical moments in one's life, it is up to the individual to decide what lesson they will ultimately learn, not the teacher. If someone wants to truly create net positive change upon the world, it requires that they be not only a student but also a teacher to themselves. In the case of Neko, he was both a brilliant learner and an even better teacher. That is what is necessary to change the world. Be like Neko and learn to change the world. •

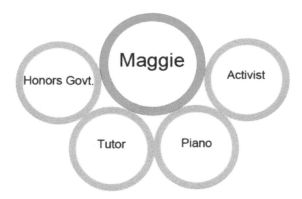

Maggie found me between classes and asked, "Unger, would you walk out of school in a protest? What would you think about a student who was instrumental in organizing a walkout?"

In the afternoon of February 14, 2018, a former student of Marjory Stoneman Douglas High School in Parkland, Florida, opened fire on students and staff. The killing spree left fourteen students and three adults dead, as well as 17 more individuals who were wounded. Many students heavily criticized the response from many of the nation's politicians in response to the Parkland shooting. President Trump offered condolences and prayers to the victims and their families. Many students asked for the leaders of the nation *not* to offer condolences but to take action that would ensure the future safety of students against school shootings. X Gonzalez, a Parkland survivor, rebuked thought and prayers... we *don't need those.*

The Women's March Youth Empowerment Organization together with the Marjory Stoneman Douglas students called for a national school walkout, one month after the shooting, on March 14th at 10:00 A.M.

Teenage activists all have one thing in common: social media. Because so many teenagers are on social media, they can use it as a way to connect and change the world. Students across the country are connecting with each other, sharing strategies, stories and anecdotes. A walkout, on the other hand, is a chance to stake out their role in this debate. Congressional leaders need to know that students can and do have very serious conversations. They can be advocates and catalysts for change. The youth of the nation are leading most of the movements and protests in America today, such as Black Lives Matter, labor movements, voting rights in Georgia, climate change across the country and anti-gun violence, among others.

I want to present students with an honest curriculum that does not hide the unpleasantries within our country's cultural, political and social history. I want to open their eyes to all that is great in the making of America, but I also want them to see the mistakes we have made and some of the terrible positions we have taken throughout history. Students help construct narratives from their viewpoints. When students spread attention about issues, the public becomes aware of these problems. These things must be addressed by the nation, because not only do they affect the existing mature adults, but they will also affect all of the future generations. *Civil engagement is the foundation of our democracy.*

There is a 1969 Supreme Court ruling related to the topic of student protest, *Tinker v. Des Moines.* A discussion about the Vietnam War

Maggie

evolved in an American History class. A day later, two young students came to class wearing black armbands to show their protest against the war. The teacher who resented their display sent the two students to the principal who suspended them because they continued to refuse to remove their armbands. Should students leave the real world at the schoolhouse door or should they be allowed to protest? In *Tinker v. Des Moines* the judges argued that students *should be allowed to protest*.

Regardless of this case decision, students can still be punished for a walkout. The administration of a school must know the whereabouts of students at all times. *Tinker v. Des Moines* was not meant to be a blanket ruling that allowed students to walk out of a class or directly out of a school. Schools are mandated to be guardians for their students. Teachers and administrators have a responsibility to keep students safe and secure while in the school environment. To take a chance and allow students to walk out of school can become a huge conflict.

"**Unger, I'd like to organize our high school for the national school walkout day on March 14th in honor of the Parkland victims.**"

"**Maggie,**" **I replied without hesitation, "I absolutely support you on the idea of a walkout. However, can I give you some advice? First, see how many students in the senior class will support you in this. The more you can involve in a positive fashion, the better. You know those students whom you can trust and who would benefit the most as the leaders of a movement such as this. Second, you need to meet with the principal of our school. I know you don't want to hear this,**"

but you need to make sure that she knows what is going on at all times because she is the person who is responsible for the safety and security of this school. Safety is paramount to her, and you'll get nothing done without her there to back you up."

Later in the week, a meeting was held in the library after school with 35 seniors, several teachers including myself, Jay Higginbotham, Terry Sorrel, and Principal Erin Dooley. The students presented their ideas for the protest and the teachers listened. We listened rather than spoke since this is the way to allow students to empower themselves and to take a stand for what they believe. The principal made the comment that if there were a student walkout, the appropriate action would be taken, and the students would undoubtedly be suspended.

"Come back to me with a solid plan of what you wish to do in this protest. Then, once you have the plan, I will contact the superintendent of Dayton Public Schools."

Ribbons made for demonstration

The students came back a few days later after they had come up with the theme for the protest, which was "Enough is Enough." The rest of the country had adopted the same theme. They decided they wanted to meet on the Stivers soccer field at 10:00 a.m. on March 14th, the same time that the protests across the country would take place. Seventeen students and teachers would meet in a small circle in the middle of the soccer field. This small group would symbolize the seventeen individuals who were killed in the shooting. The rest of the students, teachers and administrators would surround the small group making everyone aware of these problems. These things must be addressed by the nation, because not only do they affect the existing mature adults, but they will also affect all of the future generations. *Civil engagement is the foundation of our democracy.*

After Maggie gave the principal the finalized plan, the principal approached our remarkable Superintendent Dr. Elizabeth Lolli. The superintendent agreed to the protest with the understanding that the students could not leave the school building. If they wanted to have signs and walk through the hallways, they could. If they wanted to protest from their classrooms, they could. If they wanted to go to the gym, they could, but they could not leave the building itself.

When the principal came back to the students with the superintendents counter offer, the students immediately disagreed to the plan.

"We want to bring awareness to an issue. We want to show solidarity with the other students across the country that *will* be walking out. If we're just in the school building or in a classroom, we are not showing school solidarity. We need to make the protest outside the school to show the community and the country that we are walking out *with* the Marjory Stoneman Douglas students."

"To young women, I would say: Reach for the stars and believe in yourselves, and know that the only thing you can regret is not trying. A lot of success is down to luck and hard work, but it's also down to having the courage to go for it. Even if you don't know if you can do it. Even if you've never done it before. Even if you don't know anyone who's done it just shift your thinking away from 'Why me?' and instead to 'Why not me?'"

Amal Clooney

Once again, the principal met with the superintendent who after further thought, allowed the protest to occur on the soccer field. On March 10, the walkout occurred at exactly 10:00 in the morning. Between 250-300 students got up from their desks and silently walked out of their classrooms and onto the soccer field. A small group of seventeen individuals, fourteen students and three teachers stood in the center ring, surrounded by an outer ring of the balance of the students who were involved in the walkout. When a bell rang, a student in the inner circle would say the name of a student who had lost their life in the nightmare of the shooting. Then, everyone in the protest would repeat the name of the victim, and this was followed by a moment of silence. After the fourteen students' names were called, along with the succeeding moments of silence, the names of the three teachers who had been killed had their names called. These names were each followed by moments of silence. Jay Higginbotham, Benjamin Norsworthy, and I read the names of those adults.

After all of the names had been read and all of the moments of silence had occurred, there were two more bell rings with a final moment of silence. Our superintendent watched the demonstration from a distance. Others who watched from a distance were the Mayor of Dayton, Nan Whaley and two Dayton City Commissioners. Additionally, another dozen teachers attended the walkout to support the students who commemorated the lives of those who had been lost in the tragedy. *The New York Times, the San Francisco Chronicle* and a representative from WDTN *Channel Two* were present and reported on the protest for *The Nightly News*. Our Mayor, Nan Whaley, later commented on the protest at a Dayton City Commission meeting, "These young people are moving the conversation in ways that mayors and law enforcement have not been able to do."

Later in the day I asked Maggie,

"Did you achieve what you set out to do?"

"Mr. Unger, it was non-violent and it was non-political We set out to honor the victims not only of Marjory Stoneman

Douglas High School but of Columbine and Sandy Hook. Silently walking back into the building after honoring the names of those who were victims of the shooting was a very good way to respect those students and teachers."

"Do you feel anything else?" I asked.

"Unger...I couldn't help but feel a little bit upset that we couldn't do any more."

Zoe W. was one of the organizers of the protest, and she added, "Students have a voice and that matters. It doesn't matter if you're fourteen, fifteen, or sixteen, you are a person with a voice, and that's what counts."

Maggie confided in me that she agreed with what Zoe said and that the students had accomplished what they wanted to accomplish. However, she still felt that they should've done more. Maggie had always strived to better the lives of the students and adults in her life. As an outstanding pianist, she modeled for Stivers' newest piano teacher, Mr. Jeffrey Powell, in his journey to become a leader to students and musicians alike.

During the time that I knew Maggie, she had always been a firm believer in holding others accountable and driving them to better themselves personally and professionally.

A few weeks later, another student who helped organize the Stivers' walkout, Claire B., organized a demonstration at Court House Square in downtown Dayton. Claire had speakers from the University of Dayton, Wright State University, as well as other high school student speakers. They once again addressed the Marjory Stoneman Douglas tragedy.

Maggie, you learned a lot and you can really make a difference. You brought an awareness of school shootings to the community, the staff and the students. The courage and inspiration from the nightmare and the tragic loss of life at the Parkland shooting that you brought to that soccer field and the lives of everyone at the protest will always be remembered. This is what I will remember about you, Maggie. Remain an activist. ●

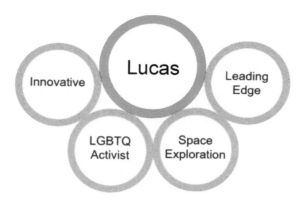

Lucas stopped me after school one day and said, "Unger, can you help me? I need some advice and support."

Lucas was the second of his family to come through my class. His older brother, Peter, was a year ahead of him and went to Ohio University after graduating from high school. Lucas was fairly quiet in class, often offering up space discoveries and facts for current events, and making the occasional remark on a topic to make light of a situation.

Coming into senior year out of the COVID pandemic, Lucas somehow managed to balance theater backstage work and consistently turned in his homework. He volunteered for "Youth at the Booth" twice, running the polls on two different election days. Lucas also coordinated the "Gay-Straight Alliance" (GSA) at Stivers, and he was always cheerful and very open about himself, openly identifying as a queer individual.

Stivers School for the Arts is a unique and exceptional environment. It has different departments and electives within each art path. The creativity and openness at Stivers allows for students to express themselves, which leads to a diverse student body. Students are from varying backgrounds and ethnicities and have varying gender and sexual identities.

Approximately, eight percent of American adults are LGBTQ+, although there are many people who may still be closeted. The number of openly LGBTQ people has risen in past years, thanks to increasing support and acceptance for these identities. Nevertheless, this doesn't mean that the queer community still doesn't have issues.

Almost half (42%) of LGBTQ youth seriously contemplate suicide, and 94% say that recent politics negatively impacts their mental health. LGBTQ youth struggle to survive and accept themselves in households that threaten to abuse or abandon them. Schools like Stivers, with an openly creative and welcoming atmosphere, are incredibly beneficial to struggling youth. Multiple students have come to Stivers from less welcoming schools and have found that their mental health was significantly better because of the more open atmosphere.

> **"It's absolutely imperative that every human being's freedom and human rights are respected, all over the world."**
> *Johanna Sigurdardotir*

However, recent state legislatures have increased these struggles, including Florida's "Don't Say Gay" bill, which demands that teachers avoid any mention of gender or sexuality in every aspect of the classroom, effectively erasing the efforts of LGBTQ people throughout history to make their voices heard.

On March 17, the Thursday before spring break, Lucas approached me with an idea. A nationwide walkout had been initiated on the social media platform, *Tik Tok*, by a user with the handle "aidyn_speaks". Open to schools across the country, the walkout was intended to protest the anti-LGBTQ legislation, like Florida's bill. Lucas, because of being president of the GSA, wanted Stivers to participate, and they had just two weeks to organize it. He sat down with me and ran through the basic plan he had created.

Lucas's proposal was very bare-bones: a set time and date (9 a.m. on April 1), with basic outlines for speakers and information. He was ready to start organizing and emailing, and once he had laid out his base plan, he was ready to move. After Lucas gained the approval of Stivers administration on the following day, four days later, he managed to meet with the superintendent, Dr. Elizabeth Lolli, who agreed to go along with the plan and even volunteered to contact the various media outlets.

The week after spring break, the GSA was "rounding third and heading for home," pulling it together the equipment, speeches and schedules for the following Friday. Multiple emails were sent out, each detailing what would occur during the walkout. I regularly checked in with Lucas, ensuring that everything was on schedule and that he was pulling it together. Each time he assured that it was, repeating that he was almost ready, as if he were reassuring himself.

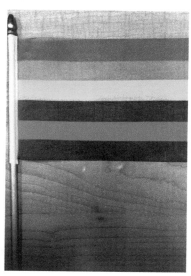

Lucas

The morning of the walkout it was cold and windy. At the end of second period, 9:05, most of the high school students and teachers walked out to the soccer field behind the school. After a few minutes of getting settled and the final sound checks, the speeches began.

Lucas introduced himself, thanking everyone who had shown up and he explained the purpose for the walkout. Lucas reminded everyone that it was not just hope that drives a movement, but action. Phoenix, GSA vice-president, rattled off a list of bills that would negatively impact the entire LGBTQ community. Other high schoolers shared their stories, thoughts and words and drove home the point that being gay or trans isn't just a fad.

The walkout lasted just over an hour, with the cold winds blowing nearly the whole time. Once the final piece had concluded, the student body filed back inside, while Lucas and Phoenix stayed behind to talk to the news' crews. That night and on the following morning, the story ran on several news channels as well as in the *Dayton Daily News*.

> **"There will not be a magic day when we wake up and it's now okay to express ourselves publicly: We make that day by doing things publicly until it's simply the way things are."**
> *Tammy Baldwin*

This walkout was the second student walkout that I've had the privilege of witnessing in my years at Stivers. The first, a somber event dedicated to the victims of the Marjory Stoneman Douglas High shooting, carried a heavy weight in its execution. Regardless of the atmosphere, it's always an inspiration to see students fight for what they believe. Struggles present opportunities. Lucas, you used this opportunity as a platform to inform fellow students and teachers about an important issue. Thank you for showing me the fighting side of the LGBTQ community and for rallying the school behind you. •

Outside the Lesson Plan

Adam • Matthew

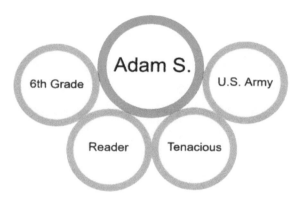

"I can't wait to read to my Book Buddy today, Mr. Unger," said Adam.

The Book Buddy program was a weekly activity that kindergarten teacher, Patty Dagget, and I had designed together. My thirty, sixth-grade students, ages 12-13, were paired with Patty's five and six-year-olds for about a half-an-hour to forty-five minutes each Friday afternoon. Both of our classes were racially diverse.

The objective of this program was to instill a love of reading and the sharing of stories between the two groups of students. I would take my sixth graders to the library to select a book for themselves as well as what would be an appropriate book for a kindergarten student. The two students could sit anywhere in the kindergarten room or in the sixth-grade classroom. They could even sit in the hallway—anywhere they could get comfortable to read to their Book Buddy. When they were finished with the book, the readers had to ask their partners some comprehension questions. Together, they would go back and look through some pictures or study how the story had developed, and the older child would see how well the younger child could answer their questions. Sometimes the kindergarten student would ask the sixth grader to read the story again, which was possible because we always had plenty of time.

Another objective was to create a variety of activities that could evolve from the reading. For instance, on holidays such as Thanksgiving or Christmas, we could draw pictures. After we had spent a number of days on the program, we could count the number of days they had worked with their book buddy. If the sixth grader had spent 50 days with the kindergartner, the older student could take the younger student and count out fifty steps together, or the sixth grader might put an outline of a shoe on the wall and the two could move the paper shoe along the wall for 50 steps. At times, we would play simple games with the kids. The program helped build reading skills as well as friendship-building skills.

At Christmas time, my sixth graders would decorate gingerbread cookies with the younger students. At these times, the kindergartner could make up a story, and my sixth-grade students would write down the story. On the last day of each year during the Book Buddy program, Patty would supply ice cream and all the fixins', and we would have sundaes together.

When my sixth grader finished reading to their Book Buddy, their culminating activity was to come back to the room and write about it in their journals. They had to write down the date they had read the book, the title of the book they had read, as well as a personal reflection of how they believed the activity had gone. This part of the activity usually took about ten or fifteen minutes weekly. I inquired one afternoon,

"What are you reading today, Adam?"

"Mr. Unger, I've got two books. I've got *The Day Jimmy's Boa Ate the Wash*, by Trinka Hakes Noble and I've got *Hue Boy* by Rita Phillips Mitchell"

"Hue Boy?"

"Yeah, Mr. Unger," Adam said, "I think it's about a little boy in Vietnam."

I replied, "Sounds great! Are you going to have time to read both of them?"

"I don't know, Mr. Unger, what do you think?"

I told him to play it by ear. "If you've got time, read both. Or you could let him choose. Let him look at the pictures and decide whichever one he feels would be more interesting to him. If you want to do both, as I've said, you'll have plenty of time."

It is absolutely undeniable that a child's reading skills are important for success in school work and life in general. Reading aloud to children has lifelong benefits which include improved cognitive development, language skills and communication. The program developed a bond between a twelve year old and a five year old. As an activity, reading improves imagination, creativity and artistic expression. It helps children socialize, it improves writing skills and it builds confidence.

The Book Buddy program gave children the ability to talk about real world situations in age-appropriate ways. The children especially enjoyed reading books about children their own age doing things that they would do in everyday life. It allowed them to point out connections in their own lives. They could note where a character was brave or courageous or if a character took a stand. They could also applaud a character who had achieved something for the first time. The book buddies would oftentimes pick out books with those types of themes.

Reading aloud to your children is the single most effective tool that we as parents and guardians can use to prepare our children for readiness in the real world. Fewer than half of the children in the United States ages five and under are read to every day, placing them at risk for reading delays and failure in school. The nurturing, one-on-one attention given to these children by their older peers in the Book Buddy program helped foster a positive association with books and a love for reading later in life.

Eventually, after leaving my sixth-grade teaching position, I transferred to a high school. At the high school, occasionally, I would have a student come up to me and say, "Mr. Unger, I don't know if you remember me, but I was in your sixth-grade class years ago, and I remember reading to a kindergarten student."

Now, a few years later, I will have students come up to me to tell me that they were read to as a kindergarten student by a student in my sixth-grade class. It always brightened my day to see that this program had such a positive and memorable impact on both my sixth-grade class and the kindergartners to whom they had read.

When I transferred to the high school, I had a freshman American History class, and I met Adam for a second time. After finishing seventh and eighth grade, he had enrolled in the school where I had been teaching.

"Mr. Unger!" he said when he first saw me again, "I didn't know you were going to be here. Can we still read out loud in class?"

"You can't use up creativity; the more you use the more you have."
Maya Angelou

When we began studying different topics, I would choose some books and have Adam read passages aloud that pertained to our subject material. I remember Adam reading selection from *I Will Fight No More Forever* about Chief Joseph and the Nez Perce War written by Merrill Beal. I also remember Adam reading selections of Elie Wiesel's *Night* when we were studying the Holocaust. He also read from *Letters to a Nation* which features a collection of letters written by normal as well as extraordinary people on topics that took place throughout American history. I can still hear Adam reading parts of Tim O'Brien's *The Things They Carried.* The other students in Adam's class always enjoyed it when he read. It ignited the flame in other students who also wanted to read aloud to *their* fellow ninth graders. And they did. They would choose books that pertained to the subject I was teaching and ask, "Mr. Unger, I have a passage that relates to the subject that we are learning, can I read it aloud?"

I would always reply, "Read it."

Ada graduated from high school with honors and wanted to be a teacher. He went on to Ohio University on a variety of scholarships. At the end of his freshman year, he ran into some financial difficulties. He did not let this stop him, and he transferred to Wright State University to major in Social Studies Education. He graduated with his degree, but instead of teaching, he enlisted in the United States Army, currently stationed at Fort Knox in Louisville, Kentucky. I ran into Adam two years ago during Christmas, and he introduced me to his wife and two of his children. I immediately asked his son,

"Does your dad read to you?"

"My dad reads to me every day!" he responded.

"Adam," I said, "thank you for your service. You're the man!"

"No, Mr. Unger, you're the man." •

"Mr. Unger, today's gonna be such a great day, isn't it? Matthew's absent!" I never expected to hear such a comment. Students typically celebrate the absence of a teacher while they mourn the absence of a classmate. But this was a different case.

The freshman class of 2000-2001 (2005 graduates) was a special class, and they were a special class for a lot of reasons. Oftentimes the graduating senior class asks me, **"Unger, which class has been your favorite."**

They always want it to be them, but I always have to be very tactful in answering that question because I never want to hurt anyone's feelings.

However, that incoming freshman class of 152 students was absolutely incredible. They were athletic, artistic, and they were academically talented when they came to Stivers in the 2000-2001 school year, and the principal said,

> **"You know, Mr. Unger, all the freshmen have a state test to take in November, and we want them to do as well as they can."**
>
> **In response I said, "You want me to teach to the test?"**
>
> **"Unger, you can do whatever you need to do to prepare these kids to pass."**

Ninety-eight percent of students passed the Social Studies test after I spent three months teaching to that test.

They were also incredibly energetic, but that's one of the characteristics of 14 and 15 year olds. Some in that class also had very strong personalities. However, they proved to be a compassionate and caring class.

Matthew sat in the first seat of the third row in my tiny classroom, a space that barely fit 35 students. Ever since I started teaching, I've always started class with, "Let's go to work. What do we have for current events today?" Every student has the opportunity to bring up news on any level or on any topic. Matthew always had something to say, and I mean *always*. If someone else tried to mention anything, Matthew would interrupt. He would always have something to add. He was never content to let another person just talk.

Once we moved on to the lesson and the day's objective, it was the same thing. Matthew was always interrupting other students and interrupting me. Sometimes a student couldn't finish their sentence before Matthew jumped in and said his piece. Another problem was that Matthew had very few friends. He'd come to school by himself, and he'd leave from class by himself. At lunch, Matthew would always be sitting alone. His locker was outside my room, and when he went home at the end of the day, he would hang out at his locker for a while, instead of leaving at the same time as the other students.

Most of the students didn't want to include him in conversations and activities because he'd take over and dominate. As a teacher, I tried so many strategies to help Matthew adjust and get along with other students. That's our job as teachers, to experiment and try everything. That's why there's an art to teaching. I could change the students' seats. I tried having them work in small groups, and I tried just moving the students around for the sake of changing them for variety, but I could get no one to work with him. I would try to sit with Matthew at lunch, just as I would sit with other students at lunch to converse with them and to learn more about them on a more social level. When I did this, it was with the hope that at least one other student would sit there as well, and take the time to talk to him, to include Matthew in their conversation.

So, on that day, when I was asked if I was glad Matthew wasn't there, I said,

"Does anyone know why he's not here? What has happened with him?"

"Unger, didn't you know that he's been suspended for 10 days?"

"I was shocked, I couldn't say anything. "He's been suspended for 10 days because…?"

"He threatened to kill another student."

They could see that I was speechless, and most of the class was laughing. Some of them even clapped. For ten days, they were going to be without someone who always dominated everything.

The class waited for my reaction, and I didn't say anything for some time. They realized that I was waiting for them to get quiet and settle down. Then I said,

"Matthew NEEDS you guys like you can't believe. He's loud, he's obnoxious and sometimes he's in your face because he wants your reaction. He absolutely needs all of you. He wants you to react to him. I repeated he needs every one of you.

How many of you have experienced foster homes? I continued. Hardly any of you. Matthew's been in and out of ten foster homes in fifteen years, one after another. No one wants him. He's not accepted by anybody. If there's a foster home that has other kids, there's always a conflict. He's never been told that he's been loved…by anyone, and he's probably never been hugged. He NEEDS each and every one of you."

"In the flush of love's light, we dare be brave. And suddenly we see that love costs us all we are, and ever will be. Yet it is only love which sets us free."
Maya Angelou

There was dead silence in the classroom.

"So I'm gonna challenge you, fifth period class, then I'm gonna challenge the entire freshman class. When Matthew returns, let him be. Let him be Matthew. Let him be loud, let him keep interrupting. I know it's not easy, because you all want a piece of the pie, but you gotta be patient, and you gotta show patience."

Later that week, I asked Andrew, Quincy, Justin, Robin, Jarrel and Joy to come to my room. We all sat in a circle, and I asked them to brainstorm some ideas to include Matthew, challenging them to take the lead.

"Why us, Unger? Why us?"

And I said, "Because all of you have strong personalities, and you're all different. I want this to come from all kinds of directions, and all of you are class leaders."

When Matthew returned, he was Matthew. At first, he was late returning, so he'd fallen way behind in his classwork. Regardless, he was still his same loud self. But by the time spring came around, there were

Matthew

some changes. He wasn't perfect, but there was some progress. He let students respond more before he butted into their conversation. Sometimes, the students included him in conversations. They would say 'hi' to Matthew in the morning. In gym, they would include him in the activities and games, and someone would usually eat lunch with him on a daily basis.

I think that once he became more included, he didn't have to fight for attention. He didn't have to 'put himself out there' every day. Each year after that, it became better. Matthew graduated in 2005 with the rest of his class.

A foster adoptive family provides a home for children to grow up in if they can't be with their biological parents. The foster system is meant to protect and nurture children, meet children's developmental needs, address delays, connect children to safe relationships and provide a safe and stable home. Today, there are more than 120,000 children and teens in foster care who are waiting for the love and security that a permanent home provides. Children enter foster care through no fault of their own. They have been abused, abandoned or neglected, and all of these children have experienced some form of trauma. Children in foster care suffer from a high rate of ill health, particularly in mental health areas. They suffer from anxiety, depression and anger.

I really believe Matthew was angry most of the time because of the variety of his living conditions and because he was continually moving from home to home.

That class of 2005, freshman class of 2000-2001, is a very special class to me. They were able to take a troubled fifteen-year old and include

105

TEACH • MICHAEL UNGER

him. They were passionate, considerate, and they tolerated Matthew even through tough times.

I ran into Matthew one day at Meijer while he was working as a cashier. I hung around until his break, and we sat and talked. I knew he was doing okay when he asked after his classmates. We ended our, conversation a handshake and a hug, and I said, **"Be safe, Matthew. You're the best."** •

The Necessity of Extra Curricular Activities

Emma • Steve

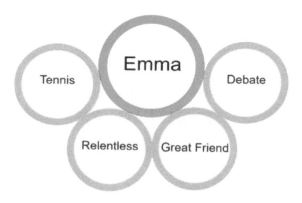

Emma said, **"We got this, Unger. We've practiced and practiced, and we are so prepared for this."**

Emma was on all three of our high school debate teams. We had a team for 2015-2016, a team for 2016-2017 and a final team for 2017-2018. I received a phone call from the district's social studies supervisor, Ryan. He asked if I could organize a debate team for the 2015-2016 school year to compete with other city schools. We were asked the previous year, but I declined for various reasons. I wanted to evaluate the commitment from the administration at our school and downtown. I also wanted to know the debate procedures that would be used.

I did some homework about the Ohio Speech and Debate Program, and I attended several registered Ohio high school debate competitions. I went to Columbus and Cincinnati for a few, strictly to observe how the debates were handled, how many debates were in a day and I wanted to determine what the overall competition was like. I did not encounter any urban public schools in any of the Ohio debates that I had attended. All the schools were private schools or wealthier suburban schools.

I responded to Ryan saying, **"Ryan, we're all in."** I offered the opportunity to seniors in my class. I didn't know exactly who to open up the program to, so I decided on just seniors. Interested seniors were to write an essay on four topics: Why do you want to join the debate team? Can you be a team player? What are your expectations about the debate program? Can you commit to the time after school?

The first year we had five talented seniors who were very good at speaking and writing, and we made one exception for a sophomore who practically begged me to be a part of the program. I told her, **"Write the essay, and we'll absolutely consider you."** The final team members were Anthony, Grade, Elisha, Isabel and Emma, the one sophomore. When Anthony graduated, he went to Ohio State, and he is now in law school. Gracie took a gap year with AmeriCorp and is now at Temple in Philadelphia. Elisha went to Sinclair, and Isabel went on to Cincinnati Christian.

"Capacity, audacity, and tenacity will take you to your mountaintop."
Robin Sharma

My second-year team was made up of James, who later went to Sinclair; Brandy, who went to Skidmore on a full scholarship; Nadja, who went to University of Cincinnati; Jacquelyn, who went to Sinclair; Sophia, who went to Ohio University; and once again, Emma, who was a junior.

The third team consisted of Tess, who went on to the University of Dayton; Zoe, who went to University of Chicago; Lydia, University of Cincinnati; Jabari, who enlisted in the Army; and Emma, finally a senior, who enrolled at Washington University in Saint Louis.

Our teams used the Public Forum Debate procedure, which was kind of new. It's made up of two teams versus two. One team debates in favor of a particular statement, while the other team argues against a particular statement. It begins with the first speaker, then a crossfire round where each side asks questions of the opposite side. After the crossfire period, the second speaker presents their argument, and then there is another crossfire round. Once all four debaters have spoken, the first speaker provides a summary followed by a 'grand crossfire.' The debate closes with a 'final focus.'

Debate Champions 2016–2017. Left to right: Jacqueline, Emma, James, Judge Walter Rice, Brandy, Nadja, Sophia.

Debate Champions 2017–2018. Left to right: Zoe, Jabari, Judge Walter Rice, Tess, Lydia, Emma.

PUBLIC FORUM DEBATE

Public Forum Debate (PF) is a team event that advocates or rejects a position posed by the resolution. The resolution is a current event and changes monthly. The pro team must uphold the resolution, and the con team must negate the resolution. A central focus of the debate is that the clash of ideas must be communicated in a manner persuasive to a non-specialist or citizen judge.

A coin toss will determine the organization of the round—generally one team will flip and the other will call, or you can flip and one team can call. The coin toss must be witnessed by you. The team that wins the coin toss shall select either: Which side of the topic they wish to uphold (Pro or Con) or which speech they would like to give (First Speech—Team A or Last Speech—Team B). The team which lost the coin toss will select from the remaining option.

Delivery is an important part of this event. Rate of speech should be at a conversational pace. Debaters should be fluent, articulate, free of slang and jargon, have good vocal variety and good eye contact with the judge. Argumentation should be organized and vigorous but civil (teams should not be obnoxious, rude or loud).

The speeches and their times are as follows:

- First Speaker (Team A) 4 minutes
- First Speaker (Team B) 4 minutes
- First Crossfire 3 minutes
- Second Speaker (Team A) 4 minutes
- Second Speaker (Team B) 4 minutes
- Second Crossfire 3 minutes
- Summary (First Speaker, Team A) 2 minutes
- Summary (First Speaker, Team B) 2 minutes
- Grand Crossfire 3 minutes
- Final Focus (Second Speaker, Team A) 2 minutes
- Final Focus (Second Speaker, Team B) 2 minutes

Prep Time (for each team) 2 minutes

While many debaters will use their own timers, it is important that you are the official time keeper and must keep track of time yourself.

Deciding the Winner

You should decide which team was most persuasive in the debate. It is best to be objective about the issues, setting aside your original opinions and attitudes. You should determine which team did the better job of debating, not which side is right and which side is wrong. Some criteria that could be considered are logical reasoning, maturity of thought, and effectiveness of communication. Additional items to consider:

- An unfair interpretation. If the interpretation is disputed by the con, it shall rest with the judge whether or not the pro is supporting a tenable position.

- Discourtesy toward opponents. Discourtesy should be penalized according to the seriousness of the offense.

- Falsification of evidence. If a team falsifies evidence in support of a point, it shall lose the point; and if the falsification is obviously deliberate, the judge shall impose an additional penalty according to the seriousness of the falsification.

- Misconstruing an opponent's arguments. A speaker who misconstrues an argument unintentionally should not be penalized more than the time wasted. If it is intentional, the team should in addition forfeit the argument.

- Introducing new arguments into rebuttal. The judges shall disregard new arguments introduced in rebuttal. This does not include the introduction of new evidence in support of points already advanced or the answering of arguments introduced by opponents.

- Speaking overtime. When a speaker's time is up, the judge shall disregard anything beyond a closing statement.

Three Debate Team Championships

Debate has been dominated for decades by elite, wealthy suburban schools, or by privileged private schools. It can be an expensive extra-curricular. Parents pay for travel to the tournaments and sometimes there is a requirement for an expensive summer institute. Students seeking entry into top colleges and universities find that a high school debate team is incredibly important, as well as being beneficial and advantageous, especially if they go on to law school. Students in urban public schools usually don't have the same opportunities.

When one considers the needs for a student to compete in a debate, a gap begins to appear between urban and suburban schools. There is a need for after school transportation, access to research and databases, a reliable internet and determined coaches. The National Association for Urban Debate Leagues has been created to address those inequalities. Today, over 22 cities and 3000 urban students have benefited from the League.

Each year we threw ourselves into the activity by learning how to construct arguments and claims and how to back them with evidence using a wide variety of sources. We had too learn if someone was trying to deflect or misdirect the conversation. The teams would watch countless videos to determine contestants' speech patterns, the quality of language, timekeeping and even 'how' to dress.

Once the League was formed, our public league schools would meet once a month for mock debates, in other words, practice. There were no judges or scoring. It was designed solely to familiarize students with the rules and format of debate, so they could become comfortable with arguing. After three practices, a championship between all of the schools that had met for the mock debates would occur the first Saturday in March.

In this run for the championship, two schools would debate against each other in the morning. During the afternoon, I would change the lineup for the participants. All of the students on each team had to know both sides of every topic and feel comfortable working with their teammates. The schools that had accumulated the most points during the morning would then square off in the afternoon for a final championship. The judges for the tournament tended to be prominent community personnel who were invited for the day. There were school board members, community lawyers, university professors, city commissioners, and even a federal district judge, the Honorable Judge Walter Rice.

Our own school was declared the champion for the first two years. We debated the following topics:

Resolved: the electoral college should be eliminated and popular vote should decide the election.

Resolved: a just government should pay reparations to indigenous populations for historic oppression.

Resolved: the United States should replace means tiered welfare with universal basic income

Resolved: civil disobedience in a democracy is morally justified

Resolved: countries must eliminate nuclear weapons arsenals

Resolved: private ownership of handguns ought to be banned in the U.S.

Our school pretty much dominated the debates for both years.

In the third year, Emma approached me just before the final in the afternoon.

"Unger, do you think Zoe and I are ready?"

I responded, "You tell me."

"We got this, Unger."

Zoe chimed in with, "We own both sides of the topic."

"I think power will come with your excellence, and people will see it."
Sherrilyn Ifill

The students really did own both sides. With the coin toss, Zoe and Emma chose the pro side of:

"United States colleges and universities should not consider standardized test in undergraduate admissions decisions."

Our superintendent officially declared our school champion after the five judges deliberated, and they presented us with our third district trophy. Judge Walter Rice once again asked us, **"How did you learn to compose your arguments so well and be able to cite so much evidence?"**

All five students wanted to chime in, but one responded with, **"That's easy, Judge! Mr. Unger has us write at least five 5Cs essays every year."**

I said, "Judge Rice, that comes from our principal, Ms. Erin Dooley, who demands rigor in all of our classrooms. She demands that every teacher in our building have their students write 5Cs essay: make a claim, back it up with evidence, and come to a conclusion."

"That is a skill that you'll take with you the rest of your life, no matter what profession you choose," said Judge Rice.

I added, "Congratulations, team. Now get that picture with Judge Rice." •

1

It had been twentyfive years since Steve and I connected, but one day, out of the blue, Steve called and asked me, "Coach, can I buy shirts for your boys' high school tennis team?"

Steve had been a strong first doubles player on the Patterson High School tennis team in 1984. During that tennis season, Steve along with many other talented players led the Patterson team to a City Championship. That was not an easy feat. Back in that day, the city league had great coaches like Ted Dooley from Belmont and Frank Riley of Meadowdale High School. Both coaches really knew the game, and, more importantly, they knew how to take raw, urban talent and develop the players into competitive athletes who could compete with any suburban school in the area. Suffice it to say, at the time, tennis was extremely competitive. When I say this, Steve and the rest of that 1984 Patterson team proved that they were like a fire in an ice box, because following their 1984 season, they ended up winning yet another city championship.

Altogether, I coached the Patterson team for thirteen years, from 1976 to 1989, and during, that time, we took home a total of three league championships, two which came from that 1984 team with Steve and the rest of his amazing teammates. Two players, Pat M., on my first boys' team, and Karen P., on my first girls' team, were the two real anchors during those first few years that I coached at Patterson. I run into Pat periodically, and he constantly reminds me that he attributes his great serve to his first year at Patterson.

Tennis Championship Team 1984. Steve is in the top row, wearing a red shirt, holding the cake. Coach Mike Unger is standing in the top row, far right.

2

After my position at Patterson, I took a temporary job at Waynesville High School, and I eventually moved on to coach women's tennis for 13 years at the University of Dayton (1992-2005). UD had a highly competitive program in a strong Division I League. Those phenomenal women had nine winning seasons, and we produced four all conference performers. They were honored five times as an 'all scholastic' team by the Intercollegiate Tennis Association. Nine of the players were honored as 'Academic All Americans'. Coaching that women's team at the University of Dayton was truly one of my proudest coaching experiences, and I am so thankful to have had that opportunity. However, my proudest coaching accomplishment of all *was* while I was *on* the court but came to affect life more *off* the court.

3

One particular day, one of my players came to me and asked if we could talk after practice. Of course, I offered to talk for as long as she wanted after the practice session was over.

Following this two-hour practice, the young lady and I met in the middle of one of the tennis courts, and we stood in the silence of the fall breeze as we started a life-changing conversation.

"Coach, I'm pregnant," she explained; "and Coach, I have an abortion scheduled for tomorrow."

I responded, albeit a little delayed, because I wanted to process my words carefully, "Who else knows? Does your mom? Your dad? Does your significant other know? Do you have a roommate that you've been able to confide in? Does anybody else know what you're dealing with here?"

"My roommate, my roommate does," she answered.

"Well, is your roommate going to go with you? What time are you scheduled for tomorrow? I asked.

She answered both of my questions with a drawn out deliberation. "Yeah, my roommate is going with me. I am scheduled at 10:00 a.m. tomorrow, Coach."

Sensing some kind of uncertainty and wanting to help in the best way that I could, I waited to respond, as I gathered the wherewithal to speak in a meaningful way. "Is it okay if we talk about that for a little bit? I don't know if you've made a final decision, but can we talk?"

"Yes," she said.

Following her answer, I began thinking of her relationship with her parents. Mentally noting memories of her with her parents who were in my office during the past spring, I asked simply, "How are things with your parents? Do you have a close relationship? You don't want to tell them?"

She easily responded, "No, I don't. I've always had this dream of playing college tennis, and I don't want this to stand in my way. I've made up my mind."

"How about your significant other? Can you tell me about him?"

"Well, we dated in high school, all through the summer. We still talk—he's at the University of Cincinnati"

I then asked, "How often do you see him?"

"Once a week, I'll go up to Cincinnati, or he'll come up here."

I said, "You don't want to let him know?"

"I don't think so."

She put the word 'think' in her answer. I felt yet again, the uncertainty in her decision. "You don't want to talk to your parents, you don't think they'll want to…"

"I don't think so, coach," she muttered.

We continued our conversation for at least another half-hour, as I wanted to make sure she was totally comfortable with what she was planning to do. Finally, after half an hour, I carefully asked, "Don't you think maybe you should call your dad? It sounds like you and your dad have an incredibly close relationship. Could you call your dad? What do you think he'd say?"

She responded, "Coach, he'd probably be up here in 30 minutes with the way he drives. It's an hour from Cincinnati to Dayton."

"If it's okay, and if you're not quite sure here, can we call your dad?" So, we did. Her dad was there in 45 minutes.

When her dad came, I told him, "I'm gonna walk away and let you and your daughter have a conversation." As I left, I also told the two of them that I would be around for as long as they were talking, *if* they wanted to talk to me. The dad looked at me puzzled as I walked away.

They walked back to me and joined me about 15 minutes later. The dad said, "Coach, I'm gonna take my daughter home."

I said, "Great, keep me posted."

He took his daughter home, and both the parents and the daughter came to a mutual agreement to withdraw her from the University of Dayton and enroll at the University of Cincinnati. This way she could be at home while she carried the baby to term. At the end of her four years, she graduated from the University of Cincinnati with her degree and with her four-year-old beautiful baby girl. Two months after graduation, she and her significant other were married.

4

I resigned from the University of Dayton years later, and when she found out, she wrote me a letter. In it she said, "Coach, I just wanted to let you know how sorry I am that you're resigning. I did not get to play for you, and I wanted to, but I always wanted my daughter to grow up and play for the University of Dayton so that maybe she could play for you.

In 2006, after I resigned from the University of Dayton, I began coaching the Stivers High School boys' and girls' tennis from 2007 to 2020. We have been the only school in the Dayton Public Schools with a tennis team, and we have been competing strictly against suburban schools. Our Stivers' team is very racially diverse, and along with the diversity, we have always been known to compete well. One of my exceptional players, Lee M., went on to compete at the Division I level in college.

In 2015, I was inducted into the Dayton Tennis Hall of Fame by the Miami Valley Coaches Association, and I will always be indebted to Jim Brooks at Chaminade-Julienne, Tim Voegeli at Fairmont and Vin Romeo at Miami Valley for their induction recommendation, and for their outstanding speeches at the induction. These three great coaches have always had high praise for my urban athletes when we came to their schools to compete.

5

Is the sport of Tennis important in an urban setting? Are all sports important in an urban public school? The answer: a resounding "HELL, YES!!"

Richard Florida is a professor and head of the Martin Prosperity Institute at the Rothman School of Management at the University of Toronto, and he maintains that the "Creative Class" is a key driving force for economic development in any society. Florida wrote a book called *The Rise of the Creative Class* (2002), and in it he cites,

> ...the three T's: Talent: being educated and skilled; Tolerance: having great diversity and a 'live and let live' philosophy; and finally, Technology. Florida believes that these three T's are... what's important... so that [we] as a society have a lot of diverse leisure activities that [can] stimulate creativity. He says, "The Creative Society" needs leisure to undertake, to enhance the area is pivotal.

The 'urban creativity' can be as simple as creating green spaces where individuals can play, bikeways for riding, tennis courts or golf fields. The need for individual sports is a pivotal force in urban life. All of these features build a real quality *of place*.

> "The Creative Class" he continues, "includes scientists, engineers, poets and novelists, and artists, entertainers, actors, designers, non-fiction writers and, most important of all, the desire to become actively involved in the places that they live."

So, is tennis important in high school? All sports are important.

6

So, I said to Steve, "I appreciate your generous offer for the shirts, but I want to meet you after all these 25 years. We haven't met since you were in high school. I would really like to get together."

We met, had a few drinks and some appetizers, and we shared the memories of our tennis teams back in the '80s.

When I presented my shirts to the athletes, I said, "Steve, one of my former tennis players is paying for these shirts; he's 'paying it forward'. It's your job, Stivers, for whoever is coaching, to follow in the generous footsteps of Steve.

Tennis "Senior Day 2021" with players, Principal Gerry Griffith, and Coaches wearing Steve's shirts.

When I often reminisce about Steve's charitableness, I also think about another great tennis player and his wise words on charity: Andre Agassi, a United States pro tennis player and an Olympic gold medalist who once said,

"Remember This. Hold onto This. There is the perfection of helping others. This is the only thing we can do that has lasting meaning. That is why we're here"

I like to emphasize Agassi's words because if we all could do something to make ourselves or someone else better, then the world *is* a better place when we help each other. That's why I'm so grateful for Steve's contributions to a budding generation of tennis players who he never met, because helping others is the only thing that lasts.

Thank you, Steve, for paying it forward. •

Engagement Beyond the Classroom

Nathan • Quincy • Maria and Neele

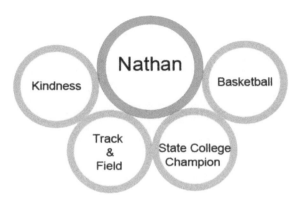

"Unger, don't forget to join me for lunch in the cafeteria today," Nathan said before leaving my class. Nathan said this to me before leaving my class.

Nathan is one of the most popular and respected students whom I have ever taught in my senior government class. He was an "A-B" student in the classroom, he always paid attention to detail and he never missed a government assignment. His parents and his older brother Ralph were tremendous role models for him. He also had a younger sister, Morgan, who just like his whole family has always pushed him to be better.

You've probably heard the phrase, 'born a leader.' Nathan was blessed with certain skills early in his life, but he learned to improve many of those leadership qualities over time. He translated these skills by offering tutoring to students who needed it after school. Nathan was very enthusiastic and passionate about sports. The characteristics that he exuded were contagious and helped him to identify problems and issues that existed on and off the school campus. He exhibited great integrity and always chose what was the right thing to do. His qualities of empathy and humility really defined Nathan, and he carried these qualities with him through the halls and especially as he entered my classroom. He was able to identify the emotions of his classmates, and he would encourage them and listen to them. He was always able to uplift his classmates' spirits. He knew how and when to be assertive, but he was always kind and he never berated anyone. He was able to evaluate and understand the misconceptions and errors of others without being critical, which is part of the reason I believed him to be so effective.

Ohio state high jump champion

He was a four-year varsity basketball player as well as being captain of the team from his sophomore year. His height of six foot five inches made his presence on the court to be known offensively and defensively. He scored in a prolific fashion, but he was also incredible at blocking and making rebounds. At times, his thunderous dunks brought spectators to their feet. Nathan was unselfish with the ball, and in addition to being the top scorer and rebounder, he also led the team in assists. Nathan was quite self-aware of his talents, but he always worked to improve himself. When the official practice was over, he would stay in the gym after everyone had left. I'd like to have a nickel for every basketball I have ever thrown to him.

On this particular day, I had asked him what we were having for lunch. "It's not what we're having for lunch, but whom we're having lunch," he replied. I grinned with a sense of curiosity, "It better be something good. I'm always up for something new."

Joining him at his table were two special needs' students. They were both freshmen who had normally sat by themselves, but Nathan wanted to include them. He could have sat at any table, with any group of students, and he would have been the center of attention, but Nathan chose to sit with these two specific students.

Nathan awarded Emmy for Camera Work.

All of us played cards together during the lunch period, and Nathan let the two young men pick out the game that they wanted to play. When the bell rang to return to class, the two boys asked Nathan if they could play cards again on the following day. Nathan told the two boys, who were smiling from ear to ear, that of course they could play cards on the next day. There seemed to be an energy that filled the lunchroom with a type of warmth and purity.

On the following day, the four of us were joined by three additional seniors, classmates of Nathan's. The seven of us continued having lunch together, off and on throughout the school year. Sometimes we would play card games, sometimes we would go the gym and shoot baskets, and sometimes we would just talk. Nathan made sure that the majority of the conversations were centered around these two specific special needs' students and what they wanted to do.

"Sometimes it takes only one act of kindness and caring to change a person's life."
Jackie Chan

One time I asked Nathan why he did this. "I'm not particularly sure," was his response. "Perhaps, I feel the need to include more diverse people in my life."

Nathan went on to take his athletics and academic prowess to Heidelberg University, where he played basketball there for four years, and one year he was named to the "First Team, All Ohio, Athletic Conference." At times, his highlights were featured on "Sports Center." Additionally, Nathan brought his talents to high jumping. In high school he had become a State Champion in Columbus. Later, he was inducted into the Stivers High School Hall of Fame. During Nathan's college experience, he competed in high jumping for all four years, and in his senior year he became the Division III High Jump Champion with a height of 2.14 meters. He graduated with a bachelor's degree in Communication Arts and specialized as a videographer. Nathan is currently working for and television station in Columbus. The last time I ran into him was at a Martin Luther King March, and he was recording the march for the television station.

All of us have an ongoing opportunity to meet new people in our lives. Nevertheless, whether we meet people professionally or personally, some people leave us with more lasting impressions than others do. Nathan, I will always remember you for your authenticity and generosity to other students at Stivers. You made the effort, and you took the time to make a difference in those boys' lives. I will never forget that.

If you want to be the best you have to do things that others aren't willing to do.
Michael Phelps

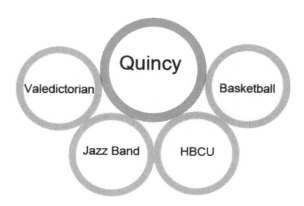

"Quincy, I know you have some tough choices ahead. I know you're thinking about your colleges for the next year. Have you narrowed down your selection yet?"

Quincy was in my American History class, and I could see from the start that he was incredibly gifted academically. He was able to answer any subject material that I would normally challenge the rest of the class with, in an extraordinary way using great depth, and in a way that the other students would want to respond and increase the conversation.

His writing skills were also great. He was able to make a claim and back it up with evidence using a variety of sources. I suggested that he use some kind of an applicable quote in his conclusion when he wrote his essays, and he always did, which added to his arguments. If I weren't quite satisfied with an answer in the room, I would often ask Quincy if there were something he would like to add, and he usually would. However, he was always humble in his replies, and in small groups, he would let other students take the lead in discussions. Sometimes he would clarify a point, but normally, he let the other group participant take charge. He made sure his classmates had been heard before he would add his own thoughts.

Quincy

I didn't have Quincy after his freshman year, but I followed him throughout his high school experience. He was a four-year member of the jazz band, and he played the trumpet. He always had the highest ranking in competitions. Additionally, he was a decent athlete, having played freshman basketball, and from his sophomore through his senior years, he played varsity basketball. In his senior year he became captain of the team. He was named Alt League First Team and All Area First Team during his senior year. He became president of the National Honor Society, and he was the Valedictorian of his class.

I went to most of his basketball games and concerts. He always caught up to me at the end of those events, with the comment, "Thanks

Unger for always supporting us," to which I replied, "Hey, part of my job, and I enjoyed it."

So, when he told me that he had decided on Alabama A&M, I immediately told him it was a great choice, but I wanted to hear how he came to his decision. I asked him if he could stop by my room some time after school that week, "I'd like to get a feel for how you came to the decision of Alabama A&M."

When Quincy stopped by, I asked him, "You could have taken your talents and abilities to Ohio State. I know you had an offer there and scholarship offers to half-dozen other schools. Why Alabama A&M?"

He told me, "Well, you know Mr. Unger, Alabama A&M has the mechanical engineering degree that I wanted. I could walk onto the basketball team and try to play there. And they also have a jazz concert band and that's something I'd like to do in my spare time."

"Hey, I like all your answers. Anything else."

"When I walked onto Alabama A&M I felt comfortable from the beginning. I just had a feel, a vibe. Unger, when you checked out Ohio University, did you have a feeling?"

"Quincy, I had a feeling from the beginning. From the very first minute, I knew that's where I wanted to go. I could feel it."

"Unger, that's how I feel about Tennessee State. Also, there's another reason I want to go there and that is Clarence. You know Clarence?"

"Yeah, I know Clarence."

"Well, he's my best friend, and he's gonna go there also. He's not able to get into some other schools, and I just want to be there to support him."

Clarence was a pretty good student, not as gifted as Quincy. He was very popular especially with his friends. Clarence had kind of a vibe that Quincy didn't have with friends. He had also been on the basketball team, but Clarence wasn't as talented as Quincy had been.

"Can I give you some advice? Alabama A&M is a great Historically Black College University (HBCU). Keep the same great attitude, if you can, that you had here at Stivers."

"What do you mean?"

"Well, you work with students here, and you involve all of them. Get involved with as many activities as you can but also support other young men there because they're going to be coming from all over the United States, and they're not going to have the background that you have. You have incredible parents, and they've instilled incredible values in you. They've nurtured and mentored you. Maybe that's what you need to do at Alabama A&M. You need to kind of follow along with that."

"I fully intend to do that, Unger."

Quincy

There are many reasons why HBCUs are important, relevant and essential to America today. The nation's 106 HBCUs only make up three percent of all American universities, but they produce 20 percent of African American graduates and 25 percent of the Science, Technology, Engineering and Math (STEM) degrees. They are a great buy. Tuition rates are on the average of 30 percent less than other comparable institutions. HBCUs provide a stable and supportive environment for students, especially for those who are at risk of not entering or not completing other four-year colleges. Low-income first-generation students may benefit from attending an HBCU. On an average, 300,000 students attend these schools. More than 70 percent of all students qualify for Federal Pell Grants and 80 percent of HCBUs receive federal loans. Lower costs can often narrow the racial or wealth gap in our country. There are 43 million Americans that have 1.3 trillion dollars in college loans. Amongst African Americans, 54 percent have college loans compared to the 39 percent of the White population. That's a disparity. Campus climate is important. A Gallup-Purdue Index [polling] noted that Black graduates of HBCUs are significantly more likely to have felt support than their Black peers from predominantly mainstream White institutions of higher learning. For more than 150 years, HBCUs have provided economic opportunities and great values. They have produced great leaders in the past and are now creating great leaders for the future. We've had students from Stivers go to Howard, Spellman, Hampton and Morehouse, just to name some of the more elite schools. However, there are many other good HBCUs out there.

"There may be people that have more talent than you, but there's no excuse for anyone to work harder than you do."
Derek Jeter

Quincy did graduate with his degree in Mechanical Engineering from Alabama A&M, and he took a six-figure income to Houston and worked in an oil refinery directly after graduation. Clarence also graduated from Alabama A&M and he followed his friend to Houston, Texas, where he went to law school. He is currently a practicing attorney. They remain close friends. ●

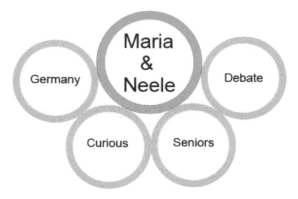

Maria and Neele came to my room one day after school. "Unger, can we talk?"

Of course, I welcomed them and gave them the chance to say what they needed to say.

"We'd like to propose a project that we think would benefit the class."

"What kind of project?"

"Can we do a presentation to the class about our native country of Germany?"

Maria and Neele were seventeen-year-old exchange students from the Frankfort area in old East Germany. They were required to take my government class when they came to this country. Though they came here for the same school year, they didn't come here together, and they had never known each other previously.

They were both great students who were always positive, earned A's and spoke incredible English. They were always prepared and willing to learn about everything America had to offer. However, they avoided topics that dealt with World War II and the history of the holocaust: here they provided less interaction.

At the beginning of each class, we discuss something from current events. The death penalty and the second amendment frustrated them. The two girls asked questions about why we have the death penalty.

To help them, I organized a debate using the rules for Ohio High School Debate and used the topic: "Should the United States Abolish the Death Penalty"? Maria and Neele took the pro side, arguing for the death penalty to be abolished, and two other students took the con side. Maria and Neele argued their side eloquently, following the rules for the debate, using the model I provided. They produced five claims using ideological beliefs of both the United States and Germany:

1. All life is valuable.

2. There is a possibility that an innocent person might be executed.

3. Each execution costs thirteen million dollars.

4. The execution of an individual is degrading within societies that respect life.

5. Twenty-three of our fifty states have already abolished the death penalty.

Both sides argued well against each other. When I stage a debate in the classroom, I provide an evaluation sheet for all of the students who are listening to the debate. Each student must fill out the evaluation, in order for the winner to be determined. Maria and Neele won the debate handily.

Thus, when they asked if they could do a project presenting information about their home to the class, I thought it was a wonderful idea. "Absolutely girls, pick a day. Let's plan your project."

> **"Wait a second, look at them. They're young people. The future is always defined by young people. We owe young people our support"**
> *Harvey Fierstein*

The girls came in after school and planned a PowerPoint presentation about their country. They wanted to include geography, religion and the differences between the two educational systems. They also wanted to include information about German writers, singers, music, food, sports and the legal drinking age in Germany. They wished to discuss Germany's immigration issues, and they wanted to bring the presentation together with some typical German foods. The menu was simple, with a meal of tradition, sausage, sauerkraut, haluska, pastas and cabbage, with cream puffs for dessert. They apologized for having no beer, since the age here is 21, and 18 in Germany. This brought a real laugh from the class.

Their presentation was fantastic. The students loved it. After the presentation, there was a question and answer period. We could ask them a question, and they could ask us a question. One student asked them about any stereotypes that they might have heard about America before they had arrived here as exchange students.

"I thought everyone was going to wear a cowboy hat," said Maria.

"I thought everyone was going to be listening to country music," Neele said.

Their answers brought many laughs.

Exchange programs create numerous opportunities for students to learn from each other. They can share and solve problems to ensure a secure future. Exchange programs create future learners who appreciate the value of international collaboration. They allow understanding and empathy, and they also create the possibility for more prosperity between participating countries, as well as the opportunity for different people to work together. Exchange programs allow employers to understand the adaptability of people from different countries, while students and families can make lifelong friends. The exchange student develops an independence previously unrealized, as they adapt to a different culture.

Maria and Neele really tried to immerse themselves into our school, while they were here. Classes had planned different events. One Saturday we went bowling. Another day we went to the mall too 'hang out' and have pizza. The senior class took Maria and Neele to the movies.

I always end the school year with a naturalization test for my government students. They are the basic questions. I want to see how my government students can perform on the U.S. citizenship test. The test is a bank of 100 questions which is offered to legal immigrants, from which they are given 10-15 questions which must be answered correctly. I give my students all one hundred questions, and they have one day in which they must complete the test. Maria and Neele did better than my American students.

Towards the end of the school year, I asked Maria and Neele what their plans were for the year after high school. Maria and Neele both said that in most European countries, students would take a gap year after completing their secondary education. So, as was common to Germany, Maria said that she would work at a kindergarten school in France, and Neele said she would work in a retirement home.

On the last day of school, some of the students brought in some gifts for the two girls. A couple of students in the Ceramics Magnet made some bowls and cups. Students from the Photography Magnet had pictures for the girls which included some of Maria and Neele. A few students brought in American flag pins. I made each girl a stained glass star so they could remember Stivers and Dayton, Ohio. I said to them, "You are two beautiful young women who have graced our class. You are incredibly great ambassadors for your country. Thank you for being here." •

Lesson Learned

Devontae

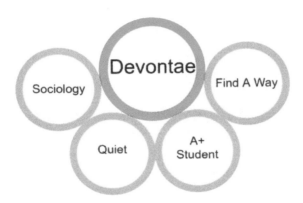

At the end of the year in my Sociology class, while all of the juniors were walking out, I said, "Looking forward to seeing all of you next year in senior Government, and I hope you're looking forward to it too."

As Devontae was walking out, I commented to him, "You were great in class. You were kind of quiet sometimes, but you were always attentive, and I hope to see all of those characteristics next year."

"You will, Unger," he said. "You will."

At that time, I was teaching five classes of senior Government and one class of Sociology, and I always compare my Sociology class to dessert at the end of a good meal. Government is the meat and potatoes, but Sociology is the dessert. It was a nice change of pace in the middle of the day, and I had a real mixture of grade levels in that Sociology class, from ninth to twelfth graders. The seniors in that class saw me twice a day. They never complained.

One of the projects in my Sociology class was a song analysis. The activity involved choosing a song that had some kind of a social justice theme. Each student had to identify the singer or the group, identify the songwriter, name the year the song came out and explain what was the social justice issue. After they had put it all together, they had to present it to the class. The presenting student would come to the front of the class, go through all of the information, and then they would read the lyrics. Once the lyrics had been read, the student could present the song in any format they preferred. Questions from the rest of the class would come after each presentation.

Devontae chose, 'What's Going On,' by Marvin Gaye. He read the lyrics, and then he played the song.

> Hey, hey-hey
> Hey, what's happenin'?
> Hey, brother, what's happenin'?
> Boy, this is a groovy party (Hey, How you doin'?)
> Man, I can dig it
> Yeah, brother, solid, right on
> What's happenin'?
> Hey, man, what's happening?
> Everything is everything
>
> Mother, mother
> There's too many of your crying
> Brother, brother, brother
> There's far too many of you dying
> You know we've got to find a way
> To bring some lovin' here today, yeah
>
> Father, father
> We don't need to escalate
> You see, war is not the answer
> For only love can conquer hate
> You know we've got to find a way
> To bring some lovin' here today

Picket lines and picket signs
DMA punish Me with brutality
Talk to me, so you can see
Oh, what's going on
What's going on
Yeah, what's going on

Mother, mother
Everybody thinks we're wrong
Oh, but who are they to judge us
Simply 'cause our hair is long?
Oh, you know we've got to find a way
To bring some understanding here today

When Devontae finished playing the song, he didn't mention the social justice issue. My initial thought was that he had overlooked it; but he didn't.

He played the video, then he asked the class, "What's this song about?" No one in the class could really get a handle on it. However, Devontae did. He said,

"It's a story told from the perspective of a Vietnam veteran, returning to the country he had been fighting for, and seeing hatred, suffering, and injustice. It's a plea for peace on earth, sung by a Man at the height of his career in 1970. It became a huge anti-war song."

I was stunned by Devontae's choice of song. I didn't present the idea to Devontae. He chose it on his own. I'm a combat veteran and that song became an anthem for most of us who were overseas. Devontae just owned the activity.

When he left the class at the end of the semester, I never saw Devontae again. He was tragically shot and killed later that summer. His friends and classmates got together at the exact place where his life was stolen, and we formed a huge circle. We chose to take turns to say prayers, sing songs, and share stories about Devontae. I shared,

"'Mother, mother, there's too many of you crying. Brother, brother, brother, there's far too many of you dying.'"

"God's dream is that you and I and all of us will realize that we are friendly, that we are made for togetherness, for goodness, and for compassion."
Desmond Tutu

Each day, 26 African American young men are killed by guns. In large cities, African Americans are killed by guns. In large cities, African Americans make up 68 percent of all the homicide victims. Even before COVID-19, another epidemic was killing our children at high rates: gun violence. Gun violence was the leading cause of death for children and teens, ages one to nineteen. In 2019, over three thousand (3371) children died because of gun violence. Nine of our children die each day, one every two hours and thirty-six minutes. Gun violence affects all of our children, but children of color and young men are the greatest risk Only 14 percent of American children are African American, but they account for 43 percent of gun deaths in our country.

Fall would have been Devontae's senior year. How would I approach this senior class, and how would we remember and include Devontae in the class?

On the first day of school, I placed a single rose in a small vase on the desk that Devontae sat in during his junior year. I also purchased a blank scrapbook. I told the students,

> **"Devontae will be with us all year, and I invite you to replace the flower every Couple of days. The scrapbook is for you to send 'D' a message: You can write in it, you can draw a picture, you can glue in pictures, it doesn't matter. They're your thoughts to him. It's how we can keep him alive."**

We celebrated 'D's' eighteenth birthday that year by having a senior balloon launched on the soccer field. Each senior decorated a balloon, and we released them simultaneously. There was laughter, there were tears, and there were stories. At the end of the year, the seniors invited his sister to their class, and we presented her with the scrapbook and a dozen roses.

Devontae, you know **"— we've got to find a way to bring some lovin' here today."** •

FACULTY PROFILES

"I've Got Your Six, You've Got Mine"

I've got the best job in the world. I'm a teacher in an urban public school system. Each day of my fifty-year career has been a gift. I've been frustrated, discouraged and I've made plenty of mistakes. I've also experienced satisfaction, success and great joy. Through it all, I've had the freedom to evolve. We should have the freedom to make a lasting impact on our students. We become inspired by the young people we teach.

"I've got your six, you've got my six" is a military phrase meaning, "I've got your back and you've got mine." I haven't traveled on this journey by myself. I've been fortunate to have been pushed and motivated by some positive mentors in my life. Who are those colleagues that we remember? We can all recall administrators and teachers who guided us. All of them had a purpose and a design.

Great urban teachers' change students' hearts. They value each student as an individual. They help students gain self-worth, acceptance and confidence.

Great urban teachers change the minds of their students, and they challenge them daily to try harder. They provide a platform for their students to constantly improve critical-thinking skills in all academic areas. They urge students to make changes and to make a difference. Urban teachers must create lessons that allow students to critically think to resolve real life issues.

The teachers and administrators that I admire have similar characteristics. They are great artists. They bring the big picture of life into the classroom so that their students can relate. Urban teachers are perceptive. They understand the socio-economic conditions that our students encounter. They are knowledgeable of their subject material and its contents. Teachers are skillful in presenting rigorous lesson plans, and they question techniques at different levels with high expectations. They strive to be highly prepared and view their lessons as documents of change, always searching for new resources to supplement their classrooms.

Highly-effective urban teachers feel a connection and a sense of duty to their students and the community. They attend the choir and piano concerts. They sit in the front row of the theater and dance performances. They applaud the student film festivals. They go to the athletic events to support teams, cheerleaders and parents. They make time to view the photo, ceramics, and creative writing programs. Students are aware of the teachers' presence and that helps to build trust. Never forget classroom-management skills. Great teachers develop their own style that brings out the best behavior and effort of the students. This is not a simple process and takes years to implement successfully.

Taking the Lead

Mr. Nazarean Mayes • Chief Erin Dooley • Mr. David Asadorian

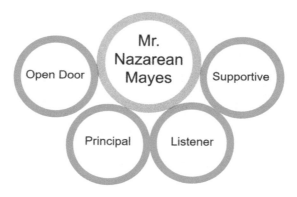

I walked into Mr. Paul Ressler's office one week after receiving my Honorable Discharge from the Army in early January of 1972. Ressler was Supervisor of Personnel for Dayton Public Schools at the time. I had been employed there as a long-term sub prior to my draft in the Spring of 1970. At that time, I had told Paul that I would hopefully return after my military service.

> "We could apply for a teacher deferment, you could probably get one, Unger."

> "Nope, I don't want to do that because I know who's fighting in that Vietnam War. Too many poor white and black people are dying over there."

Paul overheard my conversation with his secretary in the office. I was letting her know that I was back and had asked her if she could let Mr. Ressler know. Ressler heard me, "Unger, is that you? Get yourself in here!"

Mr. Nazarean Mayes

I wasn't dressed for any sort of interview. None of my clothes fit—they were too tight and too short. However, Paul said, "Welcome home, thank you for your service. I've got just the job for you. Can you start tomorrow?"

I'll always be indebted to Paul Ressler for the opportunity to teach so soon after I returned from overseas. So many of us were lost for months, even years, because we just couldn't transition from warrior to civilian. I needed to teach. Somehow, Paul knew that.

"Mr. Nazarean Mayes will be expecting you at 7:30 at Whittier School, for an eighth grade social studies position. And Unger—you'll be their third teacher in that position this year."

"You mean two teachers have already been run off?"

"Are you in, or are you out?"

"Paul, I'm all in!"

"Then I'll call Naz."

I met Mr. Mayes the following morning. This time I was wearing some of my father's clothes that fit okay and some of my own. My wardrobe wasn't very good, and I'm not a great shopper. At first, I really didn't know what Naz thought of me, since he was the first principal I had ever had the privilege of working with in my career. However, over the next few months, we developed a great professional relationship. I looked up to him for leadership and support. He grew to respect my passion for teaching and the perseverance that I brought to the classroom every day.

I'll be honest, it wasn't easy. I was a new teacher. I had some previous experience from my student teaching in Cleveland, at East High

School, but I didn't know what to expect day-to-day. The lesson planning was difficult. Some of the other teachers were old-fashioned and the discipline was challenging. It was an all African-American school, and I just didn't know what to expect. The students pushed me every day to 'bring it.' I made sure that they knew that I was coming back the next day, since they had run off the previous two teachers. I would end each class by saying, "I'll see you tomorrow."

There were several veteran teachers who really helped me. Some of them had issues of their own though, and I wish I could've leaned on them a little more. However, I was lucky, because there were some younger teachers at Whittier. We'd share stories every day, which really helped. We really tried to create an educational environment that met the needs of those students. Bruce Rahn, Eva Makstutis, and Doug Jefferies were the best. All of them went on to be fabulous urban educators in the Dayton Public Schools.

We had an assistant principal at Whittier named Mr. Scott, along with a second assistant, Mr. Williams. Mr. Scott had it out for me from day one. One of the ways students were disciplined was by paddling.

"That's right. You take a board to their backside if you have to."

"I don't. I won't paddle. I'll never do that."

"You'll never survive here or anywhere else in the Dayton Public Schools. You're way too soft," Scott commented.

Not only wouldn't I paddle, but I also refused to be a witness for other teachers when they paddled their students. Mr. Scott would also stand outside my door and listen to me teach so he could overhear how I ran my classes. Once, when I was teaching my class, I heard Naz telling Mr. Scott, "Leave the boy alone. He's gonna be a good one. The class hasn't run him off like they have the last two teachers. Let him be, Scott."

One morning while I was on my way to school during the following year, I was hijacked. I was sitting at a stoplight in front of the DeSota Bass Complex, not paying any attention. It was about 6:30 in the morning, and my window was slightly down. Just as the light changed, there was a gun at my temple. As soon as I realized what was happening, somebody jumped in on the other side and shot me once in the abdomen, as well as in both legs. I had been left in an alley in West Dayton to bleed out. All I could remember was thinking to myself, *I survived my military experience overseas, but I may not make it in Dayton.*

I crawled about one hundred yards to the front porch of an elderly woman. She phoned the police when I yelled for help, and I could hear the sirens, and the pain was becoming unbearable. A large African-American policeman pulled up in a car as quickly as he could, got out, covered me with his raincoat, and gently picked me up and placed me in the back of his patrol car. He was repeating,

"You hang on. Our ETA to St. Elizabeth's Hospital will be five minutes." He went on with this the whole drive. "ETA: four-and-a-half minutes. ETA: four minutes. My patient is bleeding from the abdomen and both legs. ETA: three-and-a-half minutes. I've got pressure on the gunshot wound but he's still bleeding. ETA: three minutes."

I blacked out. Later, when I opened my eyes slowly, I was heavily sedated, outside the emergency room, being prepared for surgery, and I saw Naz.

"Naz, how. Naz" I could barely open my eyes. "How did you know I was here? How did…"

He interrupted me, and with a huge smile, he said, "I told them I was your daddy."

I tried to laugh, but I was so heavily drugged at that point, I didn't know what to do. As I was being ushered into the operating room, Naz leaned into me, held my hand and face and whispered,

"You'll be okay. If they wanted you dead, you'd be gone. You've gotta fight with these doctors. I need you back in the classroom. You are as stubborn as hell and that's one of the

characteristics that made me know that you were going to be a great teacher. I want you back in my classroom."

"If your actions inspire others to dream more, learn more, do more, and become more, you are a leader."
President John Q. Adams

I probably returned too early, but I went back a couple of weeks later. It was difficult, but I needed to go in every day. Naz always treated me like a professional. We didn't agree all the time, but he supported me in most of my choices. He would question me a lot on how and why I would make so many home visits. I think he was worried for my safety. Sometimes he'd asked if he could come with me; and sometimes I'd ask him if he'd like to accompany me. In my career, I have made over 550 visits.

So here I am, 50 years later in my career. "I'm all in Paul Ressler. And Naz? Thank you for being 'my daddy'. A really great mentor is hard to find and impossible to forget.

Mr. Naz Mayes continued to be the principal at Whittier for several more years until he became the Director of the Industrial Arts program. He retired after 34 years. Later you could find Mr. Mayes on any golf course in Dayton, while he volunteered as a firefighter for over 20 years. ●

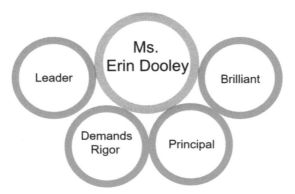

I first met Erin Dooley in early August of 2001, when I asked for and received a transfer to Stivers School for the Arts. My previous teaching experience of fifteen years was very positive. I just wanted to end my teaching career the way I began. The journey started in Cleveland at East High School teaching American History. The five years before retirement has now been twenty-two and counting. Ms. Dooley has had a great influence on my decision.

Ms. Erin Dooley

Ms. Erin Dooley began her extraordinary journey with Dayton Public Schools in 1984 teaching in the Science Department. Her first thirteen years were spent between three schools and Meadowdale High School had kept her the longest. She told me, "Although there were many challenges, I felt comfortable from the beginning. It was easy because **I** liked the kids. They were both funny and smart. I really liked getting to know them."

Ms. Dooley went from the classroom into administration. She was the principal of Stivers School for the Arts for twenty-one years. Ms. Dooley, with a dedicated staff, has led Stivers to national prominence in the arts and academics. She remarked, "I never thought Stivers needed to be turned around. I just wanted to create a place where the students and staff wanted to be." I'll never forget her saying, "Treat students in a humanizing way and create a better show in the classroom, and they will come."

If urban high schools are to succeed, quality school leadership is a crucial requirement. When schools have an effective principal, students will achieve academically. Ms. Dooley has always possessed great management and instructional leadership skills. Because of the importance of quality urban school leadership to improve academic performance, Dooley's efforts should be replicated. She creates a shared vision and sets clear goals to ensure continuous progress. She has always supported effective teachers in the implementation of high quality, standard-based instruction that results in high levels of student achievement. Ms. Dooley encourages her staff to ask,

"What are we going to do to provide each child with hope, attention, and the belief in their potential? Can we defy the odds? I knew we could from day one, and I still do."

Ms. Dooley has always provided teachers with the opportunity to engage in collaborative activities that provide for student learning. She says, "I want my teachers to have more tools for their tool box." Each year, Ms. Dooley has provided her staff with *Teaching with Poverty in Mind* by Eric Jensen, *When Gifted Kids Don't Have All the Answers* by Judy Galbraith and Jim Delisle, *Teach Like a Champion* by Doug Lemov, and *The New Art and Science of Teaching* by Robert Marzano. Ms. Dooley has never been shocked to find that urban students can achieve at high levels nor stunned to realize that her team of educators had the capacity to teach well. She has always cultivated and sustained a belief that urban educational success is possible. She does this by constantly modeling these beliefs and searching for evidence for belief.

URBAN TEACHER SURVEY

1. I have been an urban educator for _37_ years.
2. I teach _Biology, Administration_ classes.
3. Three main characteristics of urban teachers are: _resilient_ _supportive_ _forgiving_ _patient_ _enthusiastic_
4. Urban children/teens I serve are: _my favorite people on Earth!_
5. Three main characteristics of urban children/teens are: _spirited_ _driven_ _real_ _funny_ _resilient_
6. If I could change/add 2 things about urban schools/education I would _employ teachers/staff who care deeply about serving historically underserved students - getting them to a point where they can be competitive_ w/ peers across the country
7. Three mentors/colleagues that have influenced/guided me are: _Ben Kirby_ _Marla Gaskins_ _Linda Betts_
8. Five students that have influenced/guided me are: _Chenise McDaniel_ _Miles Clark_ _Isaiah Williams_ _Ivory Kennedy_ _Kayla Carson_ _Terrence Morgan_ _Vidma Watenza_ _Robert Caldwell_ _Trevon Ellis_
9. My proudest accomplishment is _Stivers School for the Arts - watching kids grow, mature, achieve - and to become competitive. Knowing that kids who graduate from Stivers have the_
Comments: _preparation needed to be successful!_

"One book, one pen, one child and one teacher can change the world."

Malala Yousafzai

Ms. Erin Dooley is always visible. She works long hours into the night and on weekends. There have been countless Saturdays and Sundays when you can find Ms. Dooley and Mr. Asadorian working on schedules, ACT and SAT testing, catching up on paperwork and contacting parents. Mr. Asadorian has said, "We work together well. There has always been a mutual level of respect." If she isn't in the hallways or the classrooms, her office door is constantly open to teachers

DAYTON PUBLIC SCHOOLS

CELEBRATING SUCCESS

Six of Dayton Public Schools' high schools held a College and Career Signing Day for seniors throughout the month of May. Students at each school shared whether they planned to attend college, enter a career, join the military or take another path after graduation, and then signed a banner to make a commitment to their future. The banners will hang in schools next year as a reminder to students to work hard.

Dayton Public Schools' Superintendent Dr. Elizabeth Lolli with Chief Erin Dooley at far left.

and students. There have been a few times when I was having some kind of issue with a student, and I would say to her, "Erin, what am I missing? Tell me about this student from another perspective." She would deliver every time. I think I miss those insights, above all, from Ms. Dooley.

> **"Leadership is about making others better as a result of your presence and making sure that impact lasts in your absence."**
> *Sheryl Sandberg*

There are literally thousands of success stories about individual students. Isaiah was a senior and in danger of not graduating. Ms. Dooley tutored him in Physical Science so he could pass a state test. If Isaiah was late, she would send Myles to retrieve him. Isaiah struggled with so many outside negative influences, but Ms. Dooley took the

Isaiah

time to recognize Isaiah's needs. He graduated and went on to play Division I basketball. Ms. Dooley would say, "No kid is a bad kid, and I always try to preserve their dignity. I'm always going to listen."

Erin Dooley is currently the "Chief" of all of Dayton's high schools. All of Dayton benefits from her ongoing compassion, her positive attitude, love of students and her sense of humor. Her reward is the respect of the students and teachers. She has always been clear about expectations. She is a crusader for excellence, integrity and perseverance. Her enduring message is that education will change lives. She does not know all of the answers, but what she does know, is that our diverse urban children need positive role models who are not afraid of the challenges and who embrace the many differences that each student brings to the classroom. Thank you, Erin Dooley, for being so inspirational in my long career. You're the best!

> **"It's the courage of the people I represent. It's my students. I see a generation that sees themselves as agents of change. That gives me hope because they are the ones we have to rely on in the future."**
> *Amal Clooney*

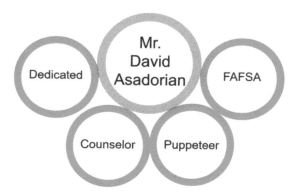

Mr. David Asadorian is quick to say "I never saw my high school coun-selor. I'm always available, and my door is open for you all the time." Mr. Asadorian has been a public school educator for 50-plus years. He began the first 17 years of his journey working as a social studies teacher for two different schools. In his first two years, he "found a home and something I really like." He has continued his career as a counselor at three different high schools. Mr. Asadorian is very proud of his accom-plishments but wants to shine the spotlight on the many students he

Bridge Award presented to Mr. David Asadorian.

Mr. David Asadorian with "Bridge" Award.

has worked with over the years.

In the 1990s, the Dayton Police Department put on puppet shows to address a variety of school issues: drugs, alcohol, bullying, gossiping, stealing, and prejudging others. Mr. Asadorian hosted their performances for several years until the police department had to discontinue them. Because Mr. Asadorian believed in the value of the outreach programs, he sought financial assistance from three different companies. Each company donated over $1,000 to buy tee shirts, puppets and transportation. Mr. Asadorian called the program: "Cougars That Care." Students audition each year to become participants, and the students and Asadorian travel to share these ideas with thousands of other students. There has been an outpouring of approval from administrators, teachers, parents and students. One grateful parent stated, "Mr. Asadorian, you saved my son: you saved him from the streets." One of his student performers, Sheldon said, "You made acting and social issues come alive for me."

> **"You have brains in your head. You have feet in your shoes. You can steer yourself in any direction you choose. You're on your own. And you know what you know you. You are the guy who'll decide where to go."**
> *Dr. Seuss*

The police department presented Asadorian the "Bridge" award for uniting segments of the city through art. When he transferred to another high school, Mr. Asadorian renamed his program, "Tigers that Care."

Mr. Asadorian relentlessly pursues students to complete the Federal Application for Federal Student Aid (FAFSA). At the beginning of November, he arranges for a representative from the University of Dayton Admissions Department to aid students with their completion and submission of their FAFSA. Stivers School for the Arts' graduating

Mr. Asadorian with Stivers School for the Arts "Tigers that Care."

Cougars with puppets: (front, from left) Jackie Tuzon, Aimee Lundee, Delisha Stewart; (center, from left) Ron Amerson, Rita Bowen, Terrence Boyd; (back) Dave Asadorian

WALLY NELSON/STAFF PHOTOGRAPHER

Mr. Asadorian with Colonel White "Cougars That Care."

classes have one of the highest rates in the region for completion. The kids have nicknamed Asadorian "Ace Money". "No kid can say that they don't or can't get money," says one student.

"Ace Money" continues his efforts by announcing several scholarships which are available each week. He brings in the forms, outlines

URBAN TEACHER SURVEY

1. I have been an urban educator for _____50+_____ years.
2. I ~~teach~~ AM A SCHOOL COUNSELOR classes.
3. Three main characteristics of urban ~~teachers~~ COUNSELORS are:
   CARING NATURE _____
   _____

4. Urban children/teens I serve are: FROM ALL WALKS
   OF LIFE
5. Three main characteristics of urban children/teens are: MORE
   MATURE / MORE RACIALY DIVERSE /
   MORE LIKELY TO HAVE READING /
   PROBLEMS
6. If I could change/add 2 things about urban schools/education I would
   HAVE A LOWER STUDENT LOAD
   LESS PAPERWORK

7. Three mentors/colleagues that have influenced/guided me are:
   JOHN NEALON
   _____

8. Five students that have influenced/guided me are:
   _____
   _____
   _____
   _____

9. My proudest accomplishment is BEING ABLE TO HELP
   A STUDENT IN SOME FORM SO HE OR
   SHE CAN PROGRESS IN LIFE.

Comments:
   BEING INVOLVED WITH STUDENTS IN
   AN URBAN SCHOOL CAN BE BOTH
   REWARDING AND FRUSTRATING.

the requirements, and announces the due dates. He also previews and reviews the material with each applying student. There is a 20-foot long bulletin board outside Mr. Asadorian's office.

> **"It belongs to the senior class. A lot of your college acceptance letters from around the country are posted on the large board for everyone to see. When visitors walk into our building, this is the first thing they see."**

Students love to point out their own letters with intense pride and joy.

On most Saturdays and Sundays, Mr. Asadorian will be in his office finalizing FAFSA applications, reviewing school material and writing recommendations. He even finds time to call parents of academically struggling seniors. His goal is to forge a successful path for each of these students. For the college bound, Asadorian wants each student to graduate college. For those seniors who wish to move forward with a career, he helps them find something that is feasible for them to survive financially. Mr. David Asadorian, you are always welcome to interrupt my class, even if it's 30 to 40 times a year, for our students. Thousands of urban public school students have you to thank for your efforts. You have said, "I'm still a dreamer after 50 years, and sometimes I get into trouble because of it." •

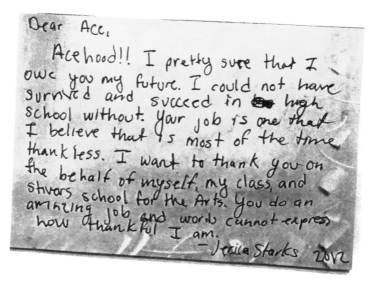

Thank you note from a parent

Art in the Heart

Mr. George Balog • Ms. Julie Anderson • Ms. DeShona Pepper Robertson

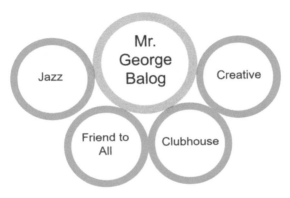

Mr. George Balog starts every class with, "Good morning, children, and thank you for coming."

Mr. George Balog

After graduating from the University of Dayton, Mr. Balog began his urban educational journey first at a high school for one year and then at two middle schools for the next 20 years as he taught American History. His final stop was the historical Stivers, built in 1908.

George, together with a passionate group of teachers and community supporters, began the concept of a new Stivers "with a vision." They saved the school from destruction and created one

John Coltrane's Gold Record

of our nation's greatest educational institutions. The school began as Stivers Middle School for seventh and eighth graders in the 1990s, and in 1996 the school added grades nine through twelve, becoming a school of seventh through twelfth graders, known as "Stivers School for the Arts".

George volunteered, "The advent of the choir, dance, creative writing, theater, orchestra and a visual arts department allowed unlimited opportunities for student creativity."

The principal, Ms. Erin Dooley, stressed the need for electives in the academic subject areas to supplement the arts. Mr. Balog suggested the study of "Jazz" within the social studies area, calling it "The History of Jazz". The class eventually expanded to include "Jazz II" and "Jazz III". Mr. Balog says, "The last 20 years of my professional career were the BEST EVER".

Mr. Balog uniquely designed these three classes after he had completed the research, the lesson plans, the evaluation process and

URBAN TEACHER SURVEY

1. I ~~have been~~ *was* an urban educator for ___45 years___ years. *American Jazz*
2. I ~~teach~~ *taught* Social Studies & 3 different sections of ___ classes. *History*
3. Three main characteristics of urban teachers are:
   dedication + commitment
   fierce loyalty
   love
4. Urban children/teens I serve are: beautiful, funny & caring kids
   inspite of some being marginalized, underserved + having limited
   resources & opportunity
5. Three main characteristics of urban children/teens are:
   strength in the face of adversity
   perseverance
   (@ Stivers) diversity
6. If I could change/add 2 things about urban schools/education I would
   A) increase funding to incentivize the best & brightest teachers to seek out urban careers
   B) include creative arts in every school
   (many more)
7. Three mentors/colleagues that have influenced/guided me are: community
   Dr. Ellis Joseph - Dean of Education at the University of Dayton
   Stivers principals Dick Penry & Tim Nealon - dreamers & schemers
   Liz Whipps - Art educator
   (Too many to mention but...)
8. Five students that have influenced/guided me are:
   Toccarra Cash
   Jonathan Cox
   Ian Boggette & Coran Henley
   Bill Bennett
   Savannah Brantley & Isaac Moore
9. My proudest accomplishment is A) having helped give "birth" to what would become Stivers School for the Art
   B) realizing a teacher's dream in designing & teaching 3 different classes on a subject I had a passion for - *American Jazz*

Comments: I would do it all over again. Once I realized I had a passion and love for the art of teaching, I never looked back. I committed myself to Dayton Public Schools & built an amazing, rewarding, challenging career. So thankful to have been a part of inspiring, dedicated staffs & Administrations. (I met my wife at one!) The give & take between teacher & student is an awesome gift!

of course the MUSIC. Then, he designed the set up for the room. In reflection, Balog said that it was always about the music and the way his students would receive the program and embrace it. His students were required to write a "Blues" song and to perform it. They would participate in "Swing Dance" lessons from a professional who George invited to the school. The students would also have to organize a New Orleans-style funeral service for Buddy Bolden, with a eulogy to be eloquently delivered. The conclusion of the service would be a party and yes, a "Dance Off." The kids would "Bust a Move" to "Feet Don't Fail Me Now" by the Dirty Dozen Brass Band.

Mr. Balog would "hook 'em" with "Jazz I" but in "Jazz II" and "Jazz III" the world of highly interesting characters, deep thinkers and enigmatic personalities would be introduced. Jazz music is an incredibly important part of American culture that has a ripple effect on nearly every aspect of American life from style and social movements to the music that came later. Balog has never hesitated to discuss racism, suicide, alcohol and drug issues in his classroom. Yes, they were and are controversial subjects, but Mr. Balog wanted to be "real" for his students. They would see the connection to their own lives through the likes of Pat Burkey, Nina Simone, Charlie Parker, Ella Fitzgerald, John Coltrane's "A Love Supreme", Miles Davis' "Kind of Blue, and Billie Holiday's "Lady in Satin," which became an integral part of many of the students' experiences.

> "Jazz music is the power of now. There is no script. It is a conversation. The emotion is given to you by musicians as they make split-second decisions to fulfill what they feel the moment requires."
> *Wynton Marsalis*

Mr. Balog always told of Abel Meeropol's poem, "Strange Fruit" that Billie Holiday performed at Café Society in 1939. Balog says,

> **"Because of the message of anti-lynching, Ms. Holiday would close her act with that song. Waiters would stop serving. The room would go dark with a lone spotlight on Ms. Holiday. She would wait up to 70 seconds with music playing before she would sing with her magical voice.**
>
> **Our students live in a complicated urban existence, and they need new hope and a sense of triumph. Balog continues, jazz is not just a style of music. It can shape our character by giving us courage, prepare us to improvise, innovate and give all of us an equal voice."**

George, the never-ending message that you brought to your thousands of students over the years will be your legacy. As you said, "If we are to move forward, we must express ourselves, and we must share our thoughts with each other?

"There are four qualities essential to a great jazzman. They are taste, courage, individuality and irreverence."

Stan Getz

Thank you, George, for coming to class every day and teaching all of us about creativity, performance and diversity. Jazz is an improvised work of art just as our lives are an improvised work of art. •

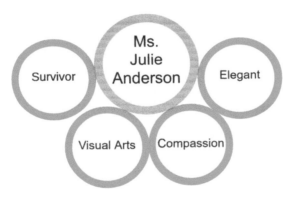

Ms. Julie Anderson is a CHAMPION for Visual Arts Education for urban students. She provides all of her students with a 'canvas' and the tools they need to become empathetic and well-rounded artists. She is dedicated to nurturing young people through every step of education. If we want the future generations to be successful, they need the skills to navigate a variety of situations. A background in visual arts provides more than just a canvas and the ability to paint; it influences how someone views the world. Ms. Anderson believes that all visual arts' students deserve the opportunity to expand their horizons and refine their creative capabilities.

Exceptional art educators possess a collection of traits that are applied, regardless of the class they teach and the mediums they use.

Ms. Julie Anderson

Oil on canvas by Julie Anderson

These traits don't just show up in a great art teacher's practice one day. Each trait is shaped and developed through intentional activities until it just becomes natural. Ms. Anderson attributes a great deal of success to her mentor and colleague Ms. Lizabeth Whipps.

Ms. Anderson wields a paintbrush and an open compassionate mind. She attended Grand Valley State University as well as Wright State University where she earned a bachelor's and master's degree in fine arts. She then became director of a gallery and obtained a second master's degree. Her particular art medium is oil on canvas or panel, and her images are primarily those of still life or landscape. Ms. Anderson became the Visual Arts Director at Stivers School for the Arts in 2011-2012. She tells us,

> **"I committed to this incredible and creative environment. My colleagues and students provide a diverse and tolerant atmosphere that is unique to this planet I want to focus on the seventh grade because I want my students to develop a strong foundation and set attainable goals and expectations. I treat each student as an artist in training."**

URBAN TEACHER SURVEY

1. I have been an urban educator for _____ 2 0 _____ years.
2. I teach _____ Visual Arts _____ classes.
3. Three main characteristics of urban teachers are: _compassionate,_ _resilient / tenacious, visionary_

4. Urban children/teens I serve are: 11-18 yrs old, 7th - 12th grade _Urban children/teens I serve are inspiring_
5. Three main characteristics of urban children/teens are: _driven (hungry for opportunity), resourceful, resilient / tenacious._

6. If I could change/add 2 things about urban schools/education I would _____
- _the Arts would be a valued part of the curriculum and provided to every student, every day._
- _Schools should not be one size fits all._
7. Three mentors/colleagues that have influenced/guided me are: _I have been very fortunate, I can't list just three!! Lizabeth Whipps, Kimm Kiser, Ernie Koerlin Diane Fitch, Bonnie Sklarski, Bill Affer, Martin Rollins_
8. Five students that have influenced/guided me are: _I + Sister Mary Magdelyn Willie Harris - didn't give up or give in Andrew Larle - turned it around, tenacious Solomon Dickerson, Clarissa Fink, Kyjaiar Watson Kevin Avila - kindness Class of 2023, when they were my 7th graders_
9. My proudest accomplishment is _____
- _Helping students see their potential and believe that they can achieve without limitation._
- _Giving young artists the opportunity to travel outside the_

Comments: _US to experience art, culture, independence, inspiration and to understand the world is so big & full of unlimited possibility_

Early on, I had the profound sense that my students were teaching me as much (if not more) as I was teaching them.

You get what you give.

She co-teaches AP art with Ms. Lizabeth Whipps and all of their aspiring artists develop a portfolio. Her students have a one-hundred percent pass rate. One very successful activity that all of the visual arts' students look forward to is "Sidewalk Chalk Day" at the end of the school year. Hundreds of students design and color a section of sidewalk in front of the school. The admiration and recognition from fellow students and the community is outstanding. Ms. Anderson's class is an

Zumbi wearing a t-shirt supporting Ms. Anderson.

Annual Chalk Day in front of Stivers School for the Arts.

open canvas where students work seriously through trial and error. She says, "Every day is a new day. You always have a new chance." The skills she teaches are observation, persistence, risk-taking, finding multiple solutions, envisioning and reflection.

It's crucial that the arts be an integral part of well-rounded and well-prepared learners and leaders. We weave the arts into our core classroom curricula as well as teach artistic skills. The integration of the arts is important because:

1. Art helps students develop creative problem-solving skills.

2. Integrating the arts with other disciplines reaches students who might not otherwise be engaged in the classroom.

3. Art experiences boost critical-thinking and teach students to take time to be more careful and thorough in how they observe the world around them.

4. Art education connects students with their own culture as well as with the wider world.

5. A report by *Americans for the Arts* states that young people who participate regularly in art classes for at least three days weekly through one full year are four times more likely to be recognized for academic achievement.

6. A study of Missouri Public Schools in 2010 found creative arts education led to fewer disciplinary problems, higher attendance rates, higher graduation rates and improved test scores.

7. Art helps students develop greater self-esteem. As students reach adolescence, their identity is often contingent upon being accepted by their peers. They begin to see themselves as artists and develop strong bonds with similarly talented peers.

8. Students of art become more resilient. They possess the ability to bounce back from adverse experiences, which is extremely important for our urban children.

One of the most important aspects of Ms. Anderson's "Open Canvas" is her compassion and advocacy for each of her students. She says, "My class is more than content." Our capacity as teachers to respond to others with compassion, is limited by our capacity to see our common humanity and our ability to understand the contexts of people's lives. There are many differences that we are able to see, such as age and body type, whereas other differences might be less visible, such as sexual orientation, mental illness and socio-economic status. Ms. Anderson is aware and open to her students. She accepts them as they are and responds to them with compassion. She creates a 'canvas' that supports inclusion and diversity, as well as equity that validates the uniqueness of everyone.

"Compassion is an action word with no boundaries."
Prince

Ms. Anderson was challenged with a different 'canvas' to paint in 2019 when she was diagnosed with cancer. She had major surgery in August and then underwent chemotherapy and radiation. She rarely missed school through October and November. She kept her students and colleagues up to date on her situation and told her students, "Don't feel sorry for me. Just know what I'm going through, and I'll be here as much as I can." She said to me,

"Don't get me wrong. My cancer was traumatic. I went through several rounds of chemo, lost my hair, and like you, the everyday radiation treatments in and out of the hospital took their toll I was overwhelmed by all of the support and love. It was transformative."

The Stivers' staff established several events to raise money to offset medical expenses. The Stivers' students raised funds by selling "Screw Cancer" tee shirts. Ms. Anderson said, "I didn't feel alone and worry whether or not I mattered." She is now in remission and taking care of her mind and body.

I know it sounds strange, but as horrible as cancer is, you become more grateful for opportunities you perhaps were unable to fully grasp. We should all welcome second chances. When you look in the mirror, you're proud of what you see, and it's not because of how your body looks, but how it feels to live inside of it.

What cancer cannot do

Cancer is so limited
It cannot Cripple love
   Shatter hope
   Corrode faith
   Destroy peace
   Kill friendship
   Suppress memories
   Silence courage
   Invade the soul
   Steal eternal life
   Conquer the spirit.

—*Anonymous*

A CHAMPION is a militant advocate or defender. A CHAMPION is a warrior and a fighter. A CHAMPION battles for rights.

Ms. Julie Anderson is a CHAMPION visual arts teacher. She has created a foundational curriculum that helps students work together and show perseverance. She has provided a "canvas" where young people feel the safest, where people feel they can be themselves. Visual arts is a fundamental component of the human experience, reflecting the world and the time in which we live. Art can help us understand our history, our culture, our lives and the experiences of others in a matter that cannot be achieved through other means. It is a source of inspiration, reflection, beauty and joy.

Thank you, Ms. Julie Anderson for being a CHAMPION who brings color, imagination and creativity to the urban community and to me. Keep on "feeding the soul."

"Our goal is to give the world a taste of peace, friendship and understanding through the visual arts, the art of celebrating life."
Steven Spielberg

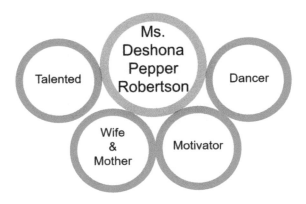

One of the "Crown Jewels" of urban public education is Ms. DeShona Pepper Robertson, Dance Department Director at Stivers School for the Arts. She transforms her studio into a home. She says, "I want to

URBAN TEACHER SURVEY

1. I have been an urban educator for *32* years.
2. I teach *Dance (all disciplines)* classes.
3. Three main characteristics of urban teachers are: *Authenticity, Energetic, Sincerity, Confidence, consistently relentless in Pursuit of Excellence + possess inner strength which sometimes comes off as intimidation.*
4. Urban children/teens I serve are: *From all walks of life...they are all beautiful...some are underserved, wealthy, middle*
5. Three main characteristics of urban children/teens are:
   - *Fear of failing*
   - *Insecurity*
   - *Seeking approval + love —an intense feeling of deep Affectio*
6. If I could change/add 2 things about urban schools/education I would *appreciate that the staff be more reflective of the student population + I would always want ART to be represented... it levels the playing field for our babies.*
7. Three mentors/colleagues that have influenced/guided me are: *Jeraldyne Blunden, Alex Robertson, T.Manuel Greene*
8. Five students that have influenced/guided me are: *Timothy Barker, Jayda Heflin, Deonna Kitwana, Jasmine Marlon, Allyia Nelloms (+Vincent Jackson)*
9. My proudest accomplishment is *simply coming to work every day making students believe that they are invinable... making them feel as though they can fly... making them feel + realize that they do not have to take the lowest hanging fruit.*

Comments: *They deserve the absolute best. WHM students SOAR + Defy Gravity!*

make them [my students] feel as though they can fly, make them realize that they do not have to take the lowest hanging fruit. They deserve the absolute best. My students know they have a place so SOAR and DEFY GRAVITY."

Ms. Pepper Robertson grew up in Chicago and attended Barat College. She continued her education at Antioch Midwest and has earned a Bachelor of Fine Arts (BFA) in dance, business and marketing, as well as a Master's Degree. When she attended a dance class and asked, "Is my name on the list?" The instructor responded, "It ought to be." To this day, if a student comes to her class she says, "You ought to be here."

#2) Dance classes
· Ballet, Modern, Dance History, Portfolio Building

#4) class, insecure, confident, gay, straight, trans-
gender, non-binary, bold, shy, consumed with
fear, abused, sweet, loved, lost, sassy,
hip, current from two parent homes, from
single family homes, raised by their grand-
mothers ... They are everything.

#6) And many more available resources.

comments:

It is simply setting the bar for my students
initially, never wavering with my
expectations and their epiphany when
they understand that they can achieve
their heart's desire and more with
· Perseverance
· Humility and
· Determination! (PHD)

Wow! This totally does it for me. The
opportunities and the doors that open
because of their hard work ...
making discipline attractive, makes
the students desire to be absolutely
EXCELLENT All of The Time.

Pepper Robertson danced professionally with the Dayton Contemporary Dance Company (DCDC) for thirteen years under the direction of Ms. Jeraldyne Blunden, the founder and Artistic Director of DCDC, the oldest modern dance company in Ohio as well as one of the largest dance companies between Chicago and New York. It holds the largest repertoire of classic works by African American choreographers in the world. The current Artistic Director is Ms. Blunden's daughter, Debbie Blunden who continues to ensure the passion, purpose and vitality for the next generation of dance artists.

Dance teacher 'a model of what she's putting into the world'

By Diane Erwin
Contributing Writer

As a dance director at Stivers School for the Arts, DeShona Pepper Robertson's curriculum is only the start of what her students are learning. "They think I'm teaching dance, but it's more than that," she said.

What she also is offering is access to opportunities, such as the ones that led her to become a principal dancer with the Dayton Contemporary Dance Company.

Robertson, 53, moved from Chicago to Dayton in 1992 to dance with DCDC, retiring in 2004 to take on a full-time role at Stivers. Part of Dayton Public Schools, Stivers accepts students in grades 7-12 via an audition process in a variety of art forms.

She teaches dance to nearly 100 students every day, also designing lesson plans and a curriculum that includes ballet, modern dance, choreography and more.

The standards are high. Robertson and her team prepare students to dance as a college major, whether or not they choose to do so. Stivers has 75 students enrolled in the dance program, and of the 15 seniors, 3 are going into dance at college – all boys. Including one who began dancing just two years ago, she said.

"But because we're pushing excellence, they're able to go into anything," she said.

She credits many of her own opportunities and success to people like Jeraldyne Blunden, DCDC's founder. As a

child, Blunden and her mother had to search for a place to train and dance because many studios didn't want to teach a Black girl.

"We stand on the shoulders of many," she said.

Poet and writer Sierra Leone nominated Robertson as a Dayton Daily News Community Gem. Leone, who has known Robertson as both a professional colleague and friend for 15 years, praised her commitment both to her students and to excellence.

A Juneteenth celebration where her students danced stands out to Leone.

As the world paused in the middle of a pandemic, her students brought movement, life and a glimpse into the future.

"It gave a light to the experience that was needed on such a greater level than I ever imagined," Leone said.

In addition to dance, Robertson teaches her students life skills like how to treat others and how they themselves should be treated, Leone said. She's a role model to her students, and the experiences she gives them and prepares them for both inside and outside of the classroom are priceless.

"She's a model of what she's putting

into the world," Leone said.

Robertson said that students rise to the standards that they are given.

"Dance empowers them to feel invincible," said Robertson, who lives in Dayton with her husband, Alex, and their 15-year-old son, William. She calls her husband, an elementary school principal, her biggest influence as an educator.

While her students at Stivers are there for dance, Robertson knows that it is also her words that affect each and every child.

"All you have to do is love the kids 1,000 percent," she said.

DeShona Pepper Robertson (left) is dance director at the Stivers School for the Arts. STAFF FILE

> "I always felt that dance was a natural part of what I wanted to express, that what I can do with my body was a part, a very important part, of me and a way to release some of those things in myself that I had been looking for."
>
> *Alvin Ailey*

DeShona Pepper Robertson encourages respect as well as respect for the body. If her students respect themselves, then they will reach out and respect others. She helps students build self-esteem through movement. Ms. Robertson applies her dance classes to what is happening in her students' daily lives. She knows that relevance and honesty is needed to understand her students. Jaya P., one of DeShona's students says,

> **"I have had endless life-changing experiences with DeShona Pepper Robertson. I've always looked up to her. I recently went through a real problem and she related her story and her message. Her capability to understand me and guide me was so important. Her dance class was a time to be vulnerable**

Ms. DeShona Pepper Robertson

Cover of application portfolio that seniors are required to submit

in a space where you are welcome. She continues to break barriers and teaches us life lessons through dance."

Pepper Robertson believes that it is always easier to put vulnerable thoughts out there if you know a connection is going to be made.

DeShona demands excellence. "There's a lot of work, but it has to be done." Her students don't want to disappoint her, and they strive so hard. Every year she gives one student, "The Dance Department's Jeraldyne Blunden Award" during the final dance concert of the year. The student who exhibits the greatest degree of persistence and determination becomes the recipient. All of her students are required to keep a journal. If they are to perform in the "Senior Showcase," they must complete a senior application. DeShona wants her students to write their story, and in return, she "...needs to understand their story." One of her younger students, Tauren, wrote the following poem for Robertson:

I twirl, I dream, I move,
Even if it's not excellent
I love, I jump
It's still not excellent
But I am free to be me.

Robertson said, "Teaching found me. I'm all about my students, and I want the spotlight on each and every one of them. That is my journey." Mr. Balog, a colleague, said "DeShona Pepper Robertson was born to do what she does." She sees that her life and her gifts are in service of the past and the future.

"Education is the most powerful weapon which you use to change the world."
Nelson Mandela

Ms. DeShona Pepper Robertson you are a LIFE CHANGING MENTOR. You are the sapphire, the ruby and the diamond of urban public education. •

Always a Teacher

Ms. Linda Betts • Mr. Douglas Jefferies • Ms. Terri Sorrell • Ms. Theresa Yoder

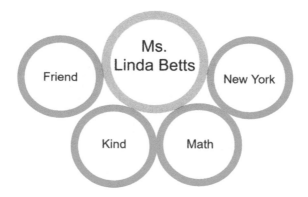

Ms. Linda Betts just never stops. She is a relentless urban educator of Dayton Public Schools. She began her journey at Fairview High School, which was a very diverse high school in 1967. For three years she taught there and then continued her career at Roth High School for eight years, teaching general science, physics and chemistry to an all African-American student population. Betts was a class advisor and developed many close personal relationships with students and colleagues. During her time at Roth, Dayton Public Schools underwent forced bussing to integrate the schools. This went from the elementary schools to the high schools. Parents and students absolutely did not want to travel across town to receive their educational needs. It disrupted continuity, and tore students from their respective neighborhoods.

Students rely on teachers to be there every day. They depend on caring adults for social and emotional needs. If those basic needs are not met, then all of education suffers. Ms. Betts continued teaching at Belmont for two years, then moved to Meadowdale for eight more years. She was an important part of the science department in both of those schools. Some of Ms. Betts' greatest memories came during the next five years when she taught in New York Public Schools. She immersed herself in the "incredibly diverse" educational and cultural environment. She survived and she thrived.

Ms. Linda Betts

The final chapter of Betts' teaching experience brought her back to Dayton, where she taught at Stivers School for the Arts. She not only taught science, but algebra as well. She and her fellow math teachers, Ms. Adrie Daniels and Ms. Terry Sorrell, have forged great working relationships, and the students are beneficiaries of the hard work. Betts provided tutoring and individual help. Sometimes I'd walk by her door and catch a glimpse of her helping two or more students long after the school hours had ended. At Stivers we often joke about Ms. Betts because of her attention to detail. School would be out at three, and she would still be there till about seven or eight at night. On weekends she would come in to make sure her lesson plans were right and that individual student needs could be met.

One day after school, one of Ms. Betts' students, Uriah, walked into Ms. Betts' class, and asked, "Would you come to our jazz band's performance tomorrow?" Ms. Betts gathered her colleagues and attended Uriah's performance the following day at a suburban high school. Uriah has a very complex stuttering issue and was hoping for emotional support. When he walked on stage, with the rest of the award-winning members, his eyes searched to find Ms. Betts, Ms. Daniels, Ms. Sorrel and Ms. Spangler. Ms. Betts said, "He waved and then commenced to perform brilliantly."

URBAN TEACHER SURVEY

1. I have been an urban educator for _45_ years.
2. I teach _Chemistry and Algebra_ classes.
3. Three main characteristics of urban teachers are:
   They view teaching urban students as a calling.
   Caring, empathetic people willing to give extra time an
   Realistic, proactive, have high expectations   effort.
4. Urban children/teens I serve are: _very dependent on schools and_
   the teachers in them for support, advice, and respect.
5. Three main characteristics of urban children/teens are: _very appreciative_
   of people who care about them (2) they view school
   as essential for their social, emotional, and educational
   needs; they want to be respected and accepted for themselve
6. If I could change/add 2 things about urban schools/education I would
   1) Shift the educational focus away from incessant,
   meaningless testing.
   2) Use electronic blocking in school buildings to eliminate use o
                                                        cell phones
                                                        during school
7. Three mentors/colleagues that have influenced/guided me are:
   Erin Dooley
   Adre Daniels
   Mike Unger
8. Five students that have influenced/guided me are:
   Nathaly Mejia (NYC)
   Lawrence Williams (Meadowdale HS)
   Mark Hall (Stivers)
   Countless other students who persevere and
   succeed despite complex social, economic, and socie
9. My proudest accomplishment is _developing the ability to forge   challenge_
   relationships with so many students over the years. I
   know that I have helped many students to see their
   own worth and realize their potential because I see the
                                                        everywhere
   Comments: _I believe that urban education is central to_
   resolving the many social, economic, ethnic, and
   racial issues that exist in American society
   today. This is because only in urban education
   are so many students able to form opinions about
   people from so many different backgrounds based on their
   own experiences as opposed to attitudes and opinions
   passed on by their parents. In an urban educational
   experience, students develop the ability to form opinions
   of people from diverse backgrounds on an individual,
   experiential basis. We as urban educators are often
   the most important influence on our students —and
   that is both gratifying and sobering. Helping students
                                                        _to_

Ms. Betts has been a great urban educator. She has stated,

"At times it has been difficult and there have been tears. The students had to know that I would be there every day for them. Once they knew that I was real and honest with them, I became more and more accepted."

Urban teaching has truly been Linda Betts' life calling.

She still returns to New York for a variety of reasons: to reconnect with friends or to go to the theater. She also wants to relive the educational experience she once had there. Sometimes she'll run into former students on the subway, and when she does, she loves recalling class assignments.

"Teachers have three loves: love learning, love of learners, and the love of bringing the first two loves together."
Scott Hayden

Linda Betts, your kindness to your students, your knowledge of your subject matter and your attention to detail will be your legacy. Those are the characteristics from you that I try to bring to my class every day. Thank You. ●

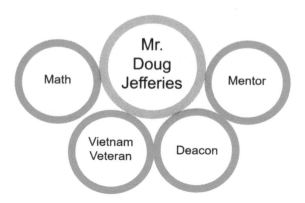

When I ventured through the doors of Whittier School in January of 1972 to begin my teaching journey, the first person I encountered in the hallway was Mr. Doug Jeffries. When we introduced ourselves to each other, there was an instant connection.

Veterans greet each other with a different kind of handshake and hug, and we knew instantly that we were veterans without saying anything to each other, and we continue to share that same feeling today, in many ways.

Mr. Doug Jeffries

Michael Unger and Doug Jeffries

Doug dropped out of a Philadelphia high school in 1965 to enlist in the Navy where he was eventually deployed to South Vietnam and served on a swiftboat along the coast for 13 months. Upon returning to the States, he earned his GED while he was still in the service. When Doug left the Navy in 1968, he discovered the Career Opportunities Program (COP) at Central State University. He said, "I discovered a new destiny."

One of the initial ten members of this program, most of them African Americans, Doug enrolled in the teacher education program which was co-ordinated by Ms. Sarah Harris and Mr. Art Thomas. In this new veteran's program, Doug was employed as a teachers aid during the day, while he could work on completing his degree in the evenings. It took him just three years.

African American men, who committed to our country, became prominent symbols associated with their service during the Civil War and later as part of the Buffalo Soldiers. The original decision that Doug made to serve our country honorably, very early in life, led him to continue to serve, however in another capacity, as an urban educator in the classroom. To teach, is to serve the community. Doug's transition out of the military changed his mission, but his unselfish commitment to mission success did not change.

Many lessons that African American male teachers bring to the classroom go way beyond academic content. It is a uniquely-lived experience that creates a richer curriculum and transfers to student success. It is a success that can be measured easily. African American teachers can provide hope, inspiration, advice, compassion and, if necessary, a really good dose of "tough love" which can make a difference.

Honoring all Vietnam War Veterans — for their — Service and Sacrifice. Thank you.

African American men make up only about two percent of all the teachers in this country, and studies show that if a black student has at least one black teacher in elementary school, they are less likely to drop out. Only seven percent of teachers across the country are African American. Yet more than half of all public school students are those of color. That is troubling.

Our students deserve a diverse teaching force to prepare them for the real world. White teachers can also benefit from having teachers of color help them with unfamiliar cultural circumstances. I knew that every time I needed advice, I could count on Doug. There was a situation with a student that didn't go very well, and Doug said, "Let's make a home visit, Unger. We'll be sitting on the front porch with his grandmother when he gets home."

This concept worked so well that it led to hundreds of home visits throughout my career. The two of us would play basketball and volleyball with the students after school. We rode bikes with them on the weekends and continued throughout the summer. Doug always said, "What we do isn't a job—it's an adventure."

Mr. Jeffries left his math teaching job at Whittier and eventually ended up at Allen School. It turned out to be a great fit for Doug's

URBAN TEACHER SURVEY

1. I have been an urban educator for _____ 32 _____ years.
2. I ~~teach~~ TAUGHT _____ MATH _____ classes.
3. Three main characteristics of urban teachers are: Compassion, Cultural Knowledge and maintain high expectations of my students
4. Urban children/teens I serve are: low income, dysfunctional families.
5. Three main characteristics of urban children/teens are: Poor attendance, insecure, Combative.

6. If I could change/add 2 things about urban schools/education I would _____

7. Three mentors/colleagues that have influenced/guided me are: Miriam Brown, Michael Unger

8. Five students that have influenced/guided me are: Ralph Middlebrooks Derwin Vance Larry Davis Floyd Jerry

9. My proudest accomplishment is be able to influence children's positive attitudes.

Comments: Being an educator will never make you rich but Seeing the young faces when they light up is priceless.

talents. He taught math, became an assistant principal, helped design the Career Education program that became nationally recognized and was featured on a *Sixty Minutes* special.

Career Education is the process of learning attitudes, beliefs, values and behaviors that are important for people to have as respectful citizens. Urban schools need to teach content knowledge that's measured on tests, but they also need to address character. Students become more attentive and more motivated to learn, according to Mr. Jeffries. They become more caring, compassionate and respectful toward their friends. Allen School also introduced a 'word of the week' throughout the years. These words included patience, caring, friendliness, helpfulness, cooperation, kindness, courage, courtesy, responsibility, optimism, tolerance, gratitude, honesty, determination, respect, community, awareness, fairness and citizenship. The teachers had to design different lessons around these character education topics on a weekly basis.

"Skills like resilience and conscientiousness can be just as important to your success as your test scores."
Michelle Obama

Mr. Douglas Jeffries retired several years ago but continues to serve. He still mentors young men whom he has previously taught. He is a deacon in his church and can be found providing transportation and food to members of the congregation. He has been a transformative figure in the lives of thousands of urban students and teachers. His adventure and legacy lives on.

Thank you, Doug, for everything I learned from you. •

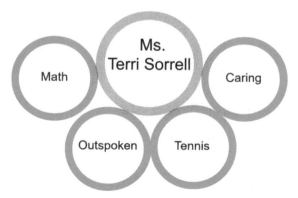

With a quick smile and a gentle voice that belies a fierce determination, Ms. Terri Sorrell always strives to support her students. Her urban teaching philosophy is, "I'm present for you?" When she walks into a classroom, it's with boundless energy and passion.

Ms. Terri Sorrell

Daniel C.-G. architecture presentation

Ms. Sorrell has been teaching in the urban public classroom for thirty years. She has a National Board Certification, and she travels the country as part of an assessment team. Ms. Sorrell currently teaches geometry and Algebra II. Previously, she has taught Probability and Statistics, U.S. History and Human Relations.

Ms. Sorrell wears many hats at Stivers High School for the Arts. She has been the senior class advisor for twenty years, scheduler for senior pictures, organizer for the senior class dinner, conductor of class elections and overseer for the graduation ceremonies. She has been the book room supervisor as well as a member of the textbook selection committee, and she has evaluated and revised the math curriculum. When she served as the math department chairperson at Stivers, she was very outspoken, and she challenged the current state and district testing requirements: "Students are chafing under the amount of time that is being taken away from their creativity, and I must sacrifice this." During the years that she has taught, she has also designed many after-school workshops. In her latest of these, she designed an architecture class where she had about twenty-five students with a professor advising her in the class.

Daniel C.-G. architecture design winner.

Sorrell believes that students deserve the best teachers that are possible and that students must serve her similarly by turning in only their best work. If she receives a paper that is not the best from a student, she returns the assignment until both of them determine it is acceptable. Her students accept her "no-nonsense approach," and they recognize that if they provide their best, they will succeed.

Mrs. Sorrell has told me, "My job is to know the students outside the four walls of my room." It is not unusual to see her grading papers as she attends piano concerts, theater events, choir performances and dancing recitals.

"If you're willing to dig deep. If you're willing to pick yourself up when you fall. If you're willing to work and work until your weaknesses become your strengths. Then you'll develop a set of skills that you can mold and apply to any situation you encounter."
Michelle Obama

Sorrell has admitted readily that she constantly learns from her students and that she is open to each of them. She told of Mark M.,

URBAN TEACHER SURVEY

1. I have been an urban educator for ___30___ years.
2. I teach __high school math__ classes.
3. Three main characteristics of urban teachers are: 1) The ability to see beyond their time and place. 2) Are present because their students need them to be. 3) Resolute
4. Urban children/teens I serve are: _deserve more._
5. Three main characteristics of urban children/teens are: 1 Want to be seen, be heard, be counted. 2 Face contradictory expectations from society 3 Want what everyone wants: happy, healthy life.
6. If I could change/add 2 things about urban schools/education I would ___
   1 Increase the number of teachers
   2 Flexible school schedules
   3 Universal, free preschool
7. Three mentors/colleagues that have influenced/guided me are: ___
   1 Rachael Murdock "If not us, who?"
   2 Adre Daniels
   3 All public school teachers with longevity.
8. Five students that have influenced/guided me are:
   1 Mark M
   2 Jayden Q
   3 Linda Sue H
   4 Dean C.
   5 My sons, Ted and Tyler. Being their mom made me a better teacher
9. My proudest accomplishment is ___ are my sons. They are kind and intelligent me who have always brought me much joy.

Comments:

Mike Unger has been an inspiration to me for years. His compassion and empathy for others has no bounds. Charismatic, Mike is always fully present. His impact on his students is far reaching and long lasting. I have been lucky to be his colleague and a privilege to be a friend.

"He represents students who taught me that what might seem insignificant to a teacher can matter deeply to a child. Beneath a prickly exterior and the 'I don't really care' attitude, students do care deeply about learning. They want to prove themselves, measure up to teacher expectations and earn the esteem of their peers."

She spoke of Jaden who was one of a number of students whose life was affected by addiction. As a sixteen year old, Jaden rode on a Saturday morning bus to participate in an audition to be accepted at Stivers. Initially, she was turned away by a volunteer because she didn't have a parent accompanying her. However, Jaden persisted in her attempt to join the Stivers' student body. She was finally spotted by a caring faculty member who recognized that other factors might be involved at Jaden's home. When she was admitted, she came to school as she could. She was responsible for her sister and herself.

"Linda Sue is another student who has taken on adult responsibilities much too young. She cares for younger siblings, aging grandparents and ailing parents." Another student, Dean, "represents students who stay true to themselves despite society's pressure to conform. LGBTQ students, students of color and student artists, all inspire me with their strength and courage."

Maggie Y., who had organized a student walkout to support the students of Marjory Stoneham Douglas High School in Florida after the shooting several years ago, had asked Ms. Sorrell for advice, "...what do you think?" "Just walk out. That's what I would do." Maggie told me that she had asked Ms. Sorrell because she had shown passion in her anger, and because of that, Maggie had always respected Ms. Sorrell's opinion and her advice.

Superintendent Dr. Lolli recently recognized Ms. Sorrell during the semi-annual "Breakfast of Champions" for her contributions to students and staff, as well as her students' high test scores. Sorrell says, "I was honored by Adre Daniels, my colleague who recommended me. Any time you get selected by one of your own peers, it's always a great compliment, and it always means so much."

Thank you, Ms. Terri Sorrell, for being present for the Stivers' students and staff. You are incredible! •

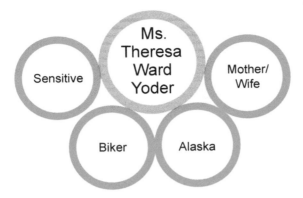

Who are the teachers that you remember? What are the things they said or did that stick with you? Ms. Theresa Ward Yoder was the first person that I met at Eastmont School after I had my initial conversation with the incredible Principal Mr. George Johnson. She greeted me in the hallway and said "I'll be teaching 5th grade across the hall from you". I was assigned to a 6th grade self-contained class. When the academic year concluded in May Mr. Johnson made the administrative decision that Theresa and I should team up and teach 6th grade together. The next sixteen years were some of the best in my professional career.

Theresa taught me the true meaning of collaboration. Both of us made teaching dynamic. We created interactive lessons together that the students still remember to this day. We would experiment constantly with class size and grouping. At times she would teach math skills to the girls and I would have the boys. The following week we would switch. Sex Education was required at the time. Again, we would re-arrange our classes so we could accommodate guest speakers and topics. Theresa would bring in cow's eyeballs for all of us to dissect. What an experience that was! How she would laugh at the students and me! I got back at her when the classes would play Elephant Ball on Friday afternoons. We would take our urban 6th grade classes, every year, to Glenn Hellen for five days to enjoy and respect nature. Let me tell you that taking sixty students away from their homes was at times, tough, but great memories.

Ms. Theresa Ward Yoder

Theresa and Mike Unger

Theresa and I set goals together. We always wanted to present a united front to our students. Strong communication built trust so that we felt confident in each other's decision making. I had to let go of my ego and let Theresa edit my ideas. She taught me that I have to allow myself to be vulnerable. Vulnerability and transparency are the birthplace of love, joy and empathy. Theresa taught me that holding tight is very safe and very small. You never know what is going to happen when you release an idea, but with the right partner it leads to bigger and better things.

Theresa always cared more about her students than the content or the classroom lessons. She was available to her students as an outlet for stress or an opportunity to talk. She allowed her students to express themselves in her classroom and through their work. What was most important to her was the total learning process, not the assessment. Her classroom was a designated SAFESPACE where students could feel comfortable to challenge ideas and create. She would spend time with students and learn about them in an extracurricular way. That is something coaches do all of the time.

"Coming together is a beginning; keeping together is progress; working together is success."

Henry Ford

URBAN TEACHER SURVEY

1. I have been an urban educator for _16_ years.
2. I teach _4-6 GRADE SOCIAL STUDIES, LANG. ARTS_ classes.
3. Three main characteristics of urban teachers are: _____
    INNOVATIVE
    FLEXIBLE
    COMPASSIONATE
4. Urban children/teens I serve are: _VERY CHALLENGING AND_
   LEARN FOR CONSISTENCY AND A SAFE ENVIRONMENT.
5. Three main characteristics of urban children/teens are: _____
    RESILIENT
    REACHABLE
    HUNGARY FOR STABILITY
6. If I could change/add 2 things about urban schools/education I would _____
   DEVELOP A MORE THOROUGH SYSTEM OF REMOVING
   DEAD BEAT TEACHERS FROM THE CLASSROOM AND
   REPLACING THEM WITH MORE HIGHLY QUALIFIED TEACHERS.
7. Three mentors/colleagues that have influenced/guided me are: _____
    MIKE UNGER

8. Five students that have influenced/guided me are: _____
    ZACH COATES

9. My proudest accomplishment is _MY FAMILY AND MY_
   TEACHING CAREER

Comments:
   WISH WE COULD CREATE MORE AFTER SCHOOL
   PROGRAMS WHERE STUDENTS GET HELP WITH
   THEIR HOMEWORK, PLAY AND JUST HANG OUT IN
   A SAFE ENVIRONMENT.

Thankfully I learned from Theresa that by seeking out admirable partners and diverse collaborators who are willing to share work, share blame, share resources and share credit you can become an exceptional urban educator. •

Above and Beyond

Mr. Randy Risner • Ms. Diana Gunckel • Ms. Bridget Federspiel

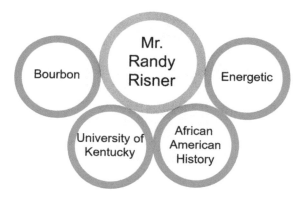

Mr. Randall Risner likes to say to his students, "You're special. Now answer me, why are you special?" Have you ever heard of the saying, "If you care about something, then you'll learn more?" It's absolutely true, and the same concept works with students. When we connect with our students on a more personal, authentic and individualized level, we build a supportive construct that empowers students to engage with the learning material more effectively. Randy Risner brings that philosophy to his classroom every day.

Mr. Risner has been a public school, urban educator for twenty years. He has been the Athletic Director overseeing all home venues, concessions and ticket sales. Randy has successfully coached the varsity softball, wrestling and soccer teams. I've always admired his dedication to his athletes and his easy way of communication. Coaching, like teaching, is an art. You bring a certain skill set to the field or court and hope the athletes will relate and respond.

Ms. Randy Risner

Mr. Risner teaches American History and African American history. He's very quick to say, 'they are one and the same'. Because Mr. Risner is empathetic, he has the ability to recognize his students' needs.

"You feel for a kid, but you don't feel sorry." Randy continues, "Students want to be seen. When we, as teachers, see them as a whole person, trust and joy are cultivated. In order to see each other, in all of its complexity, we must first work to see ourselves more clearly."

Lonnie, in Mr. Risner's eighth grade class, said,

"At the beginning of the year, Mr. Risner was out of school because of some athletic meetings. The dynamics of the class were not fully defined for the first couple of weeks. When he returned, he introduced himself and said the class would be truly able to talk and discuss all kinds of topics. He asked me to stand up, hold his hand and parade around the class with him in order to illustrate how closely linked our class would become. Mr. Risner's actions helped me so much."

Randy says, "Students want acceptance. They're not needy. Just accept who they are and what they bring to the classroom."

One of the best predictors of student engagement, effort and achievement is the relationship they have with their teacher. Mr. Risner sets high expectations for all of his students and is firm. He will, "hold the line" and refuse to accept any half-hearted effort in the classroom and on the athletic arena. Randy is quick to say, "You're going to go

URBAN TEACHER SURVEY

1. I have been an urban educator for _20_ years.
2. I teach _AMERICAN HISTORY, AFRICAN-AMERICAN_ classes.
3. Three main characteristics of urban teachers are:
   FLEXIBILITY - ABLE TO ADAPT
   EMPATHY - NOT PITY BUT CARING FOR THEM
   COMPASSION - UNDERSTANDING MANY STUDENTS ARE GOING THROUGH
4. Urban children/teens I serve are: _REALLY HUNGRY FOR_
   OPPORTUNITIES, BEAT DOWN BY SYSTEM, WANT EQUITY
5. Three main characteristics of urban children/teens are:
   RESILIANT - ABILITY TO OVERCOME
   HESITENT TO TRUST BUT WANT TO BELIEVE YOU AND TRUST YO
   WANT ACCEPTANCE - NEED TO KNOW YOU CARE AND WONT GIVE U
6. If I could change/add 2 things about urban schools/education I would
   INCREASE AFRICAN AMERICAN MALE TEACHERS
   REQUIRE CULTURAL EDUCATION FOR TEACHERS, WITH REFRESHERS
7. Three mentors/colleagues that have influenced/guided me are:
   ERIC DOOLEY
   SHANDA JONES
   GERRY GRIFFITH
8. Five students that have influenced/guided me are:
   TEARRA WEEKS
   ST. CLAIR COLE
   BRYAN JEFFRIES
   IVORY KENNEDY
   CHELSEA McGEE
9. My proudest accomplishment is _THE FACT THAT FORMER_
   STUDENTS REACH OUT AND SHARE ASPECTS
   OF THEIR LIVES WITH ME. I NEVER DID
   THAT WITH OLD TEACHERS
   Comments:
   I CAN EXPLAIN EACH OF THE MENTORS AND
   STUDENTS IF YOU WANT THAT.

places." He realizes that teachers are more than content experts and test gurus. "You have to engage students with true compassion." He knows that compassion is a learned and practiced skill, and he works to improve it every day.

> **"Love and compassion are necessities. They are not luxuries. Without them humanity cannot survive."**
> *Dalai Lama*

Long after students leave his classroom and move on to the next grade or school, Mr. Risner maintains strong relationships with them.

One of his greatest joys is "when former students reach out." He has driven countless miles to visit a student who has a need, or to be in the audience at Ohio State to render support at a dance recital. He has taken several students to their colleges to help them move. I most admire his loyalty to urban education: his students, his colleagues and our former Principal Erin Dooley. Randy has the tremendous ability to connect with anybody—that is remarkable. We won't hold his unbridled dedication to the University of Kentucky against him.

Thank you, Randy, for your friendship and support in my fight against cancer. Mother Supreme label of bourbon is headed your way. •

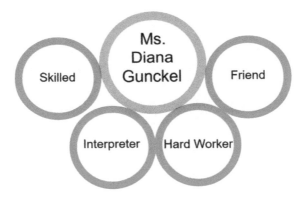

Ms. Diana Gunckel once said to me, "I never want students to feel awkward."

Ms. Gunckel is a graduate of Meadowdale High School in the Dayton Public School District. When she graduated from Meadowdale, Ms. Gunckel maintained her urban ties to Dayton by attending Sinclair Community College, a small, local school with great educational options. She initially enrolled at Sinclair with the intention of exploring a Career path in the medical field, but after a seemingly insignificant choice to take an American Sign Language (ASL) class, her whole life changed.

How many of us have ever attended some kind of theater performance, or perhaps participated in a school board meeting, or a city

Ms. Diana Gunckel

commission council meeting and our participation in the event has created a huge curve in the direction our lives went? Ms. Gunckel is an American Sign Language (ASL) interpreter and that is exactly what happened to her. The one choice in an elective course changed the events of her life.

She is among a select group of people who have the ability to communicate events like a theater performance, or a town meeting to those who are deaf or who belong to what is now known as the Deaf community. Ms. Gunckel and interpreters like her, are not performers. Each day of Ms. Gunckel's work is hard, and every minute of her presence deserves to be met with the utmost respect. Her job is to provide accessibility and inclusion to those who are hard of hearing and those who are deaf.

Communication is the very foundation of our ability to thrive in life. Millions of deaf children around the world lack the proper tools for education, and the sad reality is that a lack of education negatively impacts the quality of life those children will find as adults. Ms. Gunckel's day-to-day task is to take difficult material and not only translate it but also to deliver it in ways that make it easy to understand for students. On the most basic level, Ms. Gunckel is tasked with ensuring the future success of deaf students and that is a job unrivaled in the need for communication, and Ms. Gunckel needs to be commended for her success.

Three young women, Xashyra, Danette, and Jordan, were assigned to my senior government class. I placed all three girls in the front of my classroom with Ms. Gunckel facing them. Ms. Gunckel always worked hard to ensure that the girl understood my lectures. Oftentimes, Ms. Gunckel would leave the classroom, exhausted from her constant

URBAN TEACHER SURVEY

1. I have been an urban educator for _26_ years. *K-12 but most of my career has been*
2. I ~~teach~~ _interpret (sign language) for all_ classes.
3. Three main characteristics of urban teachers are: _hardworking! Teachers work many extra hours outside of the school day for the benefit of the students. Above and beyond "40 hours a week! Urban teachers are also caring. So many help beyond academics!_ *I would also say they are humble. Not seeking glory or praise for all they d_*
4. Urban children/teens I serve are: _unique. No two lives, situations, or paths are alike._
5. Three main characteristics of urban children/teens are: _Resilient - the adversity and experiences some of these kids have faced is hard to imagine. Resourceful and capable!_
6. If I could change/add 2 things about urban schools/education I would _make traveling available. I want all students to be able to get out of their town/city to see and experience what else is out there. Near and far! The w_ *testing is done woul_ be change Standardi_ testing, testing, a more testi_ is awful There is r "one size fits all".*
7. Three mentors/colleagues that have influenced/guided me are: _Garry Miller was a force to be reckoned with during the early years of my career. He was truly committed to his profession. I admired him_
8. Five students that have influenced/guided me are:
   Kimberly Wright
   Denise Fitzwater
   Jacob Adams
   Danette Brazil
   Michael Hurlburt
9. My proudest accomplishment is _the job I have done as a single mom. Life didn't go as planned when I was divorced when my daughter was three. Although I had friends and_

Comments: _family as huge support group, single parenting was difficult. My child was always my priority and I worked hard to do my very best as her mom. She has grown into a beautiful, strong young woman that I am so proud of. Growing up I always imagined and dreamed about being a mother. ♡ Parenting is hard but I never gave up! My greatest blessing is my daughter. So my proudest accomplishment and greatest blessing are one in the same!_

↳ personal as well. Second is Melissa Sousa. I hold in hig_ regard h_ profession ism and interpreti_ skills.

translating, and truth to told, I could not blame her. I think in part, my teaching style was the reason that Ms. Gunckel had to work so hard. It's not my teaching style to assign busy paperwork. Most of my classes consist of 'give and take' questions between the 30 students in front of me, and myself. When I would often try to steal a glance at Ms. Gunckel during class, I would always find her rapidly weaving her magic, and I could never help being anything but impressed and amazed.

As important as it was for Ms. Gunckel to communicate in order to provide skills to her students, it was equally as important for Ms. Gunckel and me to work beside each other to coordinate the dense material of a government class. Ms. Gunckel would always request my lesson plans a few days in advance. Her commitment to ensuring that she could communicate with the students was proven in her willingness to put in the extra effort and to become familiar with the materials ahead of the day of the lesson.

My job is to guarantee that students understand lecture material and homework. I use a lot of videos and segments of videos to supplement my lessons. Diana taught me the importance of closed captions, not only for those deaf students who needed to watch, but also for the rest of the students who might need a little extra aid as well.

Ms. Gunckel must also use her body language, her hands and the expressions on her face to convey the emotions and intent of the lesson. What is required of her to make the students 'feel' the emotions of what is being said, is indeed an admirable task. In using her face and body movements, the students are able to appreciate the richness of what is being said. When she does this, she ultimately elevates herself to an exceptional level of teaching.

"I am not a teacher but an awakener"
Robert Frost

Because she herself can hear, Ms. Gunckel, on a daily basis, is required to step into another world. She does so with the sole purpose of bridging the gap between the hearing and Deaf communities. It takes a lot of understanding and empathy for Ms. Gunckel to understand the nuances of Deaf culture. Deaf people really are unique in the sense that they are a distinct culture just as Americans are a distinctly different culture from the English [people from England, Scotland].

Deaf people have their own beliefs regarding what it actually means to be deaf. Some who are deaf consider deafness as a characteristic of their condition rather than a disability. Some Deaf desire that other people could be like them so they could understand their situation;

others who are Deaf, have no such desire. Furthermore, Deaf people also tend to disagree within their own community, that all Deaf should automatically be able to have cochlear implants, and many in the hearing community do not understand this reasoning. Understanding this thinking and understanding the nuances of the Deaf community are complex. Some who hear may be prone to misconceptions. Nonetheless, Ms. Gunckel works regularly to ensure that as many people as possible have an understanding of the Deaf community.

Ms. Gunckel introduced me to the rich culture of ASL. Deaf culture, as it is known, is a culture unlike any other. It has customs, so many in fact, that to list one would be an injustice to the sheer number of all of those who are deaf. Ms. Gunckel tries bridge the gap between Deaf culture and hearing culture as she tries to relay information to every type of student.

Thank you, Ms. Gunckel, for providing us with your skills and to help me gain a greater understanding of all of my students and their different ways. •

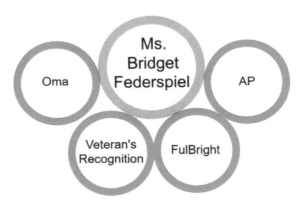

Ms. Bridget Federspiel is a professional's professional. She is a model for what aspiring urban teachers want to become. Veteran teachers also seek her advice on a wide variety of issues.

Ms. Federspiel has been with the Dayton Public Schools for the past 20 years. She has both her bachelor's and master's degree in history. She has National Board Certification (NBC), and she is also an accomplished Advanced Placement (AP) teacher for European, American and World History. Each summer she is a table leader and a reader who grades AP exams in Kansas City. She recently became a member of the developmental team that reviews the accuracy and high-standing of the AP tests.

I believe that we all have the responsibility in life to give something back, to leave the world a better place for having been here. Ms. Federspiel is a curious learner who relentlessly works to inspire her students about the world around them. She is a Fulbright Scholar who does research, completes professional projects and attends seminars around the world. She brings her knowledge and experiences back to the students as she sheds some light on real life and controversial issues.

In 2019 Ms. Federspiel received a Fulbright Distinguished Award, and she was selected for a three-month residency program in Vietnam where she traveled and taught and studied at the university level. Her objective was to observe today's Vietnamese people and their society and to research their cultural changes since 1975. She describes the Vietnamese as a warm and welcoming community, a culture that is forward-looking and interested in the United States.

In the summer of 2021, as a Fulbright Scholar, Ms. Federspiel attended a three-week seminar that was hosted by Kent State University, in an examination of the reason for the 1970 shooting tragedy when the National Guard took the lives four promising Kent State students during a Vietnam War protest.

Additionally, Ms. Federspiel serves on the Dayton Council of World Affairs (DCOWA) and the Junior Council of World Affairs

Ambassador Tony Hall and
Ms. Bridget Federspiel

(JCOWA). One of her duties is to plan the annual DCOWA meeting. In the Spring of 2022, DCOWA presented the Dayton Peace Prize to Ambassador Tony Hall. The Academic Quiz Bowl, held each year at the University of Dayton, is organized and directed by Ms. Federspiel, and her Stivers team always competes well. She always encourages her students to participate in National History Day, and she spends countless hours evaluating those projects.

> **"Ideal teachers are those who use their service as bridges over which they invite their students to cross and then encourage them to create bridges of their own."**
>
> *Nikos Kazantzakis*

One of Ms. Federspiel's goals is to visit and experience as many UNESCO World Heritage sites as possible. She has already visited the Great Wall of China, Machu Picchu and the Old Havana District of Cuba, just to name a few. One of her latest journeys was to the Cahokia Mounds east of St. Louis. The mounds are the largest pre-Columbian settlement north of Mexico with over 120 mounds. The Dayton Foundation gave a grant to Ms. Federspiel so that she could take her entire class to Mammoth Cave National Park. She applies for these grants because she wants her students to share in the significance of these places, and she wants each of her students to increase their scientific knowledge.

On top of her vast array of accomplishments, Ms. Federspiel designed a veterans' project whereby her students are able to interview veterans of all wars and conflicts. Hundreds of her students have conducted over 550 interviews that have been archived in the Library of

Dayton Daily News
Complete. In-Depth. Dependable.

Area teacher helps veterans tell their wartime memories

Ms. Bridget Federspiel with Dayton Daily News article about veterans.

Congress. Her "Valentines for Veterans" program has received regional recognition. Veterans from the Dayton area are invited to come and spend a few hours talking about their military and life experiences. Between these two programs, students can share with the vets the moments of impact in their careers. In this way, students from seventh through twelfth grades get the opportunity to know real American heroes. Ms. Federspiel challenged her Advanced Placement history class to research former Stivers' young men who gave their lives in Vietnam in service to America. They are:

James Huntley, Michael Pattaw, Joe Calvin Paul, Philip Baugh, J.D. Walters, Thomas Eugene Hoover

All six who gave their last full measure were honored during Memorial Day services in 2022 at the Dayton Vietnam Memorial Park. Ms. Federspiel and her class are going to recognize these fallen heroes with a plaque at Stivers School for the Arts.

Staff Sergeant Melvin Morris Congressional Medal of Honor Awardee at Stivers School for the Arts.

The Stivers' student body heard messages from Congressional Medal of Honor Awardee, Staff Sergeant Melvin Morris, a veteran of the Vietnam War, and Cindy LaPointe Defier, the wife of Congressional Medal of Honor Awardee, Joseph LaPointe. In conjunction with the veteran's project, Bridget traveled to England, Germany, Japan, South Korea and Normandy, in a quest to bring more veterans' stories back to her students to keep their memories alive. As an adjunct professor at Wright State University, she inspires other teachers in her class to address veterans' issues and to discuss the needs of veterans as they return home.

"We remember those who were called upon to give all a person can give, and we remember those who were prepared to make that sacrifice if it were demanded of them in the line of duty though it never was. Most of all, we remember the devotion and gallantry with which all of them enabled a nation as they became champions of a noble cause."

Ronald Reagan

Ms. Federspiel is omnipresent for her fellow teachers. She helps teachers update their state licenses, and she works with the Dayton Education Association (DEA) to negotiate contract issues. On the last day of every year, she presents retiring teachers with flowers.

She somehow has also found time to be an inspirational athletic coach, and her seventh and eighth grade volleyball teams have always competed for league titles. Federspiel's knowledge of tennis and her own ability to play at a high level, makes her an excellent coach for the boys' and girls' varsity tennis teams at Stivers.

Bridget Federspiel is an inspirational urban educator who knows the importance of shaping the lives of our young people and laying a foundation from which they might soar. It's an incredible thing, the human spirit. It's a reminder of the powerful role we can play in someone else's life.

Thank you, Ms. Federspiel, for your professional excellence. •

Courage to Face the Future

Mr. Ivory Kennedy ● Mr. Michael Unger

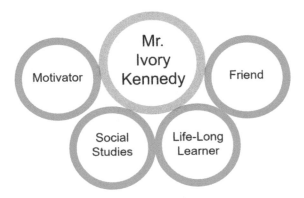

"Unger, I always knew I could count on you. When I entered the parking lot of Stivers each day, every morning I would look for your car. When I saw it, I knew it would be a good day. I felt so relieved because you were never absent. That's the attitude that I wanted the students to have about me. They gotta realize I'm there for them 24/7."

After his graduation from our high school, Mr. Ivory Kennedy received his education degree from Ohio State University. Currently he is working on his master's and his Ph.D program while he is Program Manager of the Middle Childhood Education Program at Ohio State University and is the summer coordinator at the Metro school in Columbus, Ohio, part of Ohio State. Formerly, Mr. Kennedy worked for three years at the Freedom School at the Boys and Girls Club of Dayton where he and his staff tirelessly prepared Dayton youth for school. Ivory served on the equity and diversity committee, and was the lead eighth grade teacher. He was also selected to be part of the committee which is developing a model for the Metro school in order to promote a partnership with the Columbus Public Schools. He is the lead eighth grade teacher of his TOT (Teacher Based Team). As if that's not enough, Mr. Kennedy coordinates an annual trip to Washington D.C. He is extremely dedicated to the success of these trips. He recently contacted Ohio Congressman Tim Ryan and Franklin County City Commissioner John O'Grady about underwriting a portion of the school trip expenses, and this was a monumental success.

Mr. Ivory Kennedy

Mr. Kennedy is a former student of mine, and now he is a professional colleague and an incredible friend. We recently visited together and discussed a wide variety of topics: Leticia James, the Attorney General of New York, the case against Donald Trump and the recent, "Don't Say Gay" bill that has been initiated in Florida. We chatted about our inclusion of Emmett Till in our curriculum and the differences between our methods and talking points. He's having his eighth graders read ten different articles about Till before they write a reflection paper. My class also watches *The Murder of Emmett Till,* and then they write a paper.

We talked about current events, comparing our thoughts about the health crisis in America and its effect on our students. Ivory is keenly sensitive about how the COVID crisis has impacted his students, making them further behind in their studies.

On January 6th, 2021, when dissenters rioted on Capitol Hill, catching the nation by surprise, Ivory called me and said, "Mr. Unger, tomorrow can we get our classes together and have a virtual discussion? I feel like this is a conversation that needs to be had with our students."

URBAN TEACHER SURVEY

1. I have been an urban educator for _____5 years_____ years.
2. I teach _American Studies I + II   1491 – 1877_ classes.
3. Three main characteristics of urban teachers are: _____
   1. Passionate
   2. Self-less
   3. Gritty
4. Urban children/teens I serve are: _Worthy of the opportunity._
5. Three main characteristics of urban children/teens are: _____
   1. Triumphant
   2. Determined
   3. Relevant
6. If I could change/add 2 things about urban schools/education I would_____
   • Mandate that all teachers were required to attend PD about Social Justice and implement it in their curriculum.
   • Involve + invite parents to attend classes for them to maintain engagement.
7. Three mentors/colleagues that have influenced/guided me are:_____
   • Michael D. Unger
   • Randal Risner
   • Dr. Augustine and Conlee Ricketts (OSU program directors)
8. Five students that have influenced/guided me are:_____
   • Gene Sutton
   • Zeyad Boyce
   • Kia Perez
   • Claire Coleman
   • Keon Stone
9. My proudest accomplishment is_____
   Making it through college and continuing to provide education to children that look like me!

Comments:
_____Education is an optional field that students have no choice to participate in. As educators, we have to make students see the value in their participation and how it can pay off in their futures. _____ Because they are worth it.

I said, "Absolutely."

During our call, our classes talked together for about an hour. His kids had the floor first, and my students followed. I feel they learned a lot from each other. It was a great experience. Every time we talk, I learn something from Ivory.

"Unger, you taught me to have patience and to see each student's potential so that they can overcome their

circumstances. I put myself in the position to listen to their stories and to help them push through. Just like you listened to us and helped us push through."

The last thing Ivory wanted to talk about was an ongoing problem that he was having with one of his students.

"Mr. Unger, I'm having a problem with one of my students, and I don't know if I'm getting enough support from my administration," he said. "This student confronted me saying I talk too much about Black Lives Matter and that I talk too much about the issues surrounding it."

"Well how did you deal with that?"

"I told him it was a part of the history lesson, but I don't think he thought that was a satisfactory answer."

So I gave Ivory some advice about how he could share his thoughts and feelings with students in a constructive, creative and educational way. I walked him through the type of questions he could ask the student and what kind of assignments he could create to help all of his students better understand all of the material being taught and how it was still relevant

"I'm for truth, no matter who tells it I'm for justice, no matter who it is for or against."
Malcolm X

After solving all the worlds problems, something that usually takes us two to three hours, our conversations conclude with Ivory saying: "Love you, Unger." I always reply right away and say, "Love you too, Ivory."

Mr. Kennedy brings so much promise to the field of urban education. He has high expectations of his students and his colleagues. He's passionate about life and his career. Ivory, when you share these thoughts with me, I know the future of urban educators is in great hands. When you have such high expectations of yourself, you care. The sky is the limit and you're going to continue to be a great teacher and administrator. •

Looking back, the **LIGHT** went on when I enrolled at Ohio University in the fall of 1966. To be completely honest, I went to college for just two reasons: to play college baseball and to avoid the draft (the war, and Vietnam). Coach Wren at Ohio University gave me the opportunity to walk on as a pitcher. He was aware of my skills in Dayton, but he could not give me a scholarship until I could prove myself as a freshman.

When I turned eighteen, the Selective Service draft lottery identified my birthday as 120 of 365. The war in Vietnam was escalating extremely fast under the Johnson administration, and birthdays under 200 would be called to serve our country in the Army, unless there were some kind of deferment. United States' universities were overwhelmed with record enrollments as young men desperately tried to escape the conflict. Educational deferments were provided for full-time students taking a minimum of 12 credit hours; then the Armed Services would not touch you. I figured the war would be over by the time I graduated in the next four years, especially considering the length of our previous conflicts.

The **LIGHT** almost went out during October of my first college semester. My sociology professor offered extra credit to any student who would give up a Saturday, ride five and a half hours on a bus to Tennessee and register people to vote. At the time, I didn't know about Selma, one of the most important protests of the Civil Rights Movement in the '6os, nor did I know about the Voting Rights Act of 1965. I simply presumed that every citizen had the opportunity to vote. Because of my middle-class white background and the high school attended, I had never discussed anything controversial nor dealt with any type of racial issues.

The bus ride through Kentucky was uneventful, just small talk between the 35 of us that were willing to go to Tennessee. When we crossed the Kentucky border, I saw a sign that read, "Welcome to Tennessee", and on both sides of the interstate were Tennessee State troopers. It looked odd, but I did not think much of it at the time. When we arrived at the bus station of a small town about an hour later, I immediately knew better. Waiting for us was a large crowd, all white, with about ten police cruisers behind them. What happened next is almost unfathomable to comprehend and much of it I don't even remember and that's probably a good thing.

When the bus came to a halt, out came the Confederate flags, rocks pelted the bus and the hate slogans were too numerous even to count. The bus windows were broken, and, before we knew it, someone threw a bottle filled with lighted gasoline through a broken window. It exploded, spread everywhere and the front exit became blocked. I grabbed the girl across the aisle from me by her red hair and headed for the rear door of the bus. When I burst out of rear door, for a split second, I thought we might make it. At the instant of our exodus, some-one hit me with a club or a bat, and then I only remember awakening two days later in the hospital with severe lacerations and a concussion. Later, someone told me about the bus, which was totally destroyed, and I saw some pictures. Some students suffered burns, smoke inhalation, bruises and cuts... but all of us had survived. Within a two-week period, most of us were back in class at Ohio University, but I never again saw the red-haired girl who I had snatched from the bus. I did hear that her father had come all the way from Pittsburgh to take her out of school.

A month later, the sociology professor, with an 'okay' from the university, asked if anyone wanted to try a different town in Tennessee to register voters. I was the first to volunteer, without any hesitation, but I asked if I could bring a bat. On this second round, I registered over 500 people. It was a huge success, and there were no altercations this time around. I ended up taking four different sociology classes from that professor, a man who ended up becoming one of my mentors.

The **LIGHT** went on again at the beginning of my sophomore year. I had taken an education class as an elective, and I was given the opportunity to tutor students at a local Appalachian high school. During the evening, once a week, I would tutor two to four students simultaneously. I loved it! I helped them with both reading and math, and I was 'hooked'. Right away I declared education as my major with a focus in social studies.

The **LIGHT** was ever so bright when I disembarked from a Greyhound bus in Cleveland on a very cold day in early January of 1970. I continued on a city bus, east on Euclid Avenue to East 79th Street. From there I walked 20 blocks to East High School, where I met the school's principal, and my supervising teacher for my student teaching experience. I was fortunate enough to rent an apartment (which was really just a room) about three blocks from the school, where the owner, an older woman, practically adopted me for the next three months. The school, whose nickname is *The Blue Bombers*, became my new home away from home. Teaching American History every day to 180 students became the very center of my world. I learned so much, and it was there that I knew that urban teaching was going to become my vocation.

I had to become my own fiercest advocate to student teach in urban Cleveland. The majority of education students at Ohio University were placed in rural areas within a 30-mile radius of Athens, Ohio. A small minority of students received suburban student teaching experience. The argument that I constantly had to confront with my student teaching office, was the concern for my safety and security in the urban area of Cleveland. The office was made up of three professors, who I had to convince that I was able to manage my own welfare I had to counter the stereotype of violence that was attached to the city. I raised *uncomfortable* eyebrows when I *demanded* that they find an OU professor who would ultimately have to evaluate my teaching performance in the urban district. Finally, an education professor who had taught two of my classes, offered to drive the four-hour trip to Cleveland every two weeks so that he could evaluate my class teaching. He was incredibly supportive, and, fortunately, it eventually it led to the placement of other university students who wanted to teach in an urban district as well.

The **LIGHT** dimmed considerably after my student teaching when I returned to the university. The entire school had been sent home because of the anti-Vietnam war demonstrations which occurred on and around campus. We received our diplomas in the mail. Two weeks later, I received my draft notice. I could have applied for a teaching deferment but elected not to pursue it. I knew that a disproportionate number of low-income white and black individuals were fighting and dying in that unjust conflict.

I was sent to Fort Leonard Wood for basic training. My company of approximately 300 men was created as a by-product of emptying the Philadelphia jails. These men could choose either incarceration or military service. We were then assigned to Fort Ord, California, for Advanced Infantry Training (AIT for thirteen weeks. I was deployed to South Korea and was attached to a Republic of South Korea (ROK) Army Infantry Regiment. We were in and out of Vietnam *all the time*. The LIGHT was almost extinguished multiple times.

"For the most part they carried themselves with poise, a kind of dignity."
Tim O'Brien, The Things They Carried

When I returned to the United States through Fort Lewis Washington, I requested my one-way ticket home to take me through San Francisco. I wanted time to decompress, redefine and focus before I brought my "military baggage" back home. I wanted to find some of the **BRIGHT LIGHT** I had left thirteen months before.

Arriving in San Francisco was difficult. People said things to me that no one should ever have to hear. As I walked through the airport, people looked at my uniform and immediately judged me negatively. I took a taxi to the YMCA, checked in and immediately went to a used clothing store. I bought some slacks—too short. I bought a shirt—too tight. I bought some sneakers—too big. But hey, at least it wasn't a military uniform with the insignia that defined my rank and tour of duty.

I proceeded to Union Square, a public plaza bordered by Geary, Powell, Post and Stockton streets. Within this one block plaza and the surrounding area, is one of the largest collections of department stores, up-scale shops, art galleries and hotels in the United States, making it a major tourist destination and local meeting place.

I just wanted to sit on a wall, soak up the sun and blend in for the first time in over a year, I closed my eyes for a couple of minutes and woke up to laughter everywhere. Sitting next to me was a mime wearing a very colorful striped tee shirt, tight trousers, rainbow suspenders and a face painted white. Every movement I made, he copied. I tried to walk away, he followed. My pants were up high, he pulled his up in imitation. The response and laughter from the hundreds of people gathered around made me believe that he had done this multiple times each day.

After about five minutes, I sat on the wall and he sat next to me. I thought okay *I can play this game*. I gave him a hug, he hugged back. I kissed him on the cheek, he kissed back. The crowd went bananas. The **LIGHT** was so bright. I was home. After a little while, he left me to pursue an unsuspecting woman in the crowd. Little did I know, until several years later, that the mime was Robin Williams delivering his own unique persona.

The **LIGHT** was brilliant when I returned to Dayton that January. Within two months, Mr. Paul Ressler, Director of Personnel for Dayton Public Schools, placed me in an eighth-grade social studies position, teaching at Whittier School. I married my college sweetheart, Yolanda Paska, in mid-March, and we began our urban teaching journey together. She was an *incredible* speech therapist. We mutually agreed that this was our time to become the very best urban professionals possible. She devoted an incredible amount of time participating in educational workshops and sharing with colleagues, creating games in the evening and writing individual performance objectives. She purchased *countless* children's books for her students, and her attention to detail was one of the greatest attributes she possessed. Each evening we would share our stories. Sometimes they would end in laughter, sometimes tears but always in exhaustion. The journey started in 1972 and culminated in the first week of March in 2019.

The **LIGHT** dimmed during a slice of this period when our daughter, Emily, was born six weeks premature. Seeing her with so many tubes sustaining her heart and lungs at Childrens Hospital was devastating for Yolanda and me. We juggled teaching and the hospital. Nonetheless, our daughter was *never* alone. One of us was always with her. We were so lucky to have Dr. Daniel Conforti as our pediatrician. One day when I arrived at the neo-natal intensive care unit (NICU) to see Dr. Conforti in a rocking chair, massaging Emily's heart. "Unger," he said "we need to talk. You need to tell me a little bit about your background."

When he discovered my military service, he gave me six journals with articles about Agent Orange to read. This was 1983, and scientists were just discovering how deadly the defoliant used in the Vietnam War was. Little did I know that nearly 40 years later, my life was going to be threatened with two types of cancer because of that deadly chemical.

The **LIGHT** was incredibly bright one day after school when I went to see my wife at the hospital. She was rocking our daughter *without any tubes*. I simply collapsed next to the empty incubator as Dr. Conforti sat next to me. We took Emily home a week later.

The **LIGHT** almost went out when I was assaulted and shot three times on my way to school one day. Fortunately, I had outstanding support from surgeons, my principal (Nazarene Mays), my colleagues, my wife and *all* of my fantastic students that I was teaching at the time. They could not understand my need to keep teaching them, which pushed me to come back right away. Although coming back as early as I did was too soon, I needed their support as much as they needed mine.

The **LIGHT** dimmed in November of 2018 when Yolanda was diagnosed with metastatic breast cancer just before Thanksgiving of that year. I wanted to resign from teaching, but my principal, Erin

Yolanda Unger and daughter Emily

Dooley, would *not* think of it. Yolanda also didn't want to hear my resignation talk.

"We'll work with you, Unger," Ms. Dooley insisted, "and your classes will work with you also. We will take care of it. You'll need as much normalcy as possible with what you're about to go through."

I didn't know I could do such a disservice to my class because I didn't know how much school I would be missing. Ms. Dooley wanted me at Stivers. My senior class of 2019 was also understanding, compassionate and supportive.

Yolanda was my absolute priority. I was her primary caregiver. It's like a friend, former colleague and coach, Ted Dooley once said, "Unger, when we married, that's what we signed up for."

The cancer progressed very rapidly, and the chemotherapy was destroying Yolanda.

I had to take Yolanda to the hospital for some tests. A massive blood clot was found between her heart and right lung. She was rushed to Emergency Intensive Care. After three days of care and tests a team of eight doctors concluded that Hospice was the next step. The next ten days were so very difficult. On the seventh day we were holding hands. I wouldn't let her go. She took both of my hands and said, "Michael, you need to write a book. You have so many amazing stories to tell of your experiences in urban schools. Your exceptional students need to have their unique stories told, too. Tell me one more..."

So, I told her Justin's story. After the story, still holding her tightly, she said, "I want to go home. I'll be waiting for you."

She slipped away. Four months after the initial diagnosis, and the **LIGHT** that was always there, was now gone. Somehow, I found the strength in Yolanda's courage to return to teaching a week later, My students were my safety net. The class of 2019 will always be one of my most special because of their unwavering and unconditional support.

> **"We never lose the people we love, even in death. They continue to participate in every act, thought, and decision we make."**
>
> *Leo Buscaglia*

I revisited San Francisco in December of 2020. I wanted to retrace, redefine and recapture some of the magical moments I had all those years ago and make more memories with help from an incredible friend. I rediscovered China Town, world class museums, incredible restaurants, the Redwoods, Golden Gate Park and Bridge, Mission Dolores and Union Square where I had sat with Robin Williams. The **LIGHT** was coming back.

In Loving Memory …
Yolanda M. Unger

"I'm an ordinary person who found herself on an extraordinary journey."
"There's power in allowing yourself to be known and heard, in owning your unique story, in using your authentic voice. And there's grace in being willing to know and hear others. This, for me, is how we become."

~Michelle Obama from *Becoming Michelle Obama*

Yolanda M. Unger

Wife, Mother, Daughter, Sister, Teacher, and Friend, born in Hamilton, Ontario, Canada. Passed away peacefully at Hospice of Dayton with husband Michael at her side on Wednesday, March 6, 2019 after a courageous and heroic battle with an aggressive form of Breast Cancer and its complications. She was a graduate of the Marion Franklin Class of 1966 in Columbus. She pursued her college education at Ohio University, Class of 1970, with her degree in Speech and Hearing Therapy. She retired from the Dayton Public Schools Auxiliary Services Program, but continued teaching part time at Immaculate Conception School. She was passionate about working with her colleagues, devoting time, inspiring and encouraging her students and giving to all a positive attitude. She loved to spend time sewing dresses for girls in Africa, gardening, and baking pies. Yolanda is survived by her husband of 46 years, Michael; daughter Emily; mother Hendrina C.J. Lamers Paska; sister Gail (Ted) Wille; brother Christopher; and nieces and nephews. Family will receive friends Friday, March 15, 2019 from 5-6:30 pm with a reflection of Yolanda's life by Michael and Gail at 6:30 pm at the Tobias Funeral Home, Beavercreek Location, 3970 Dayton Xenia Road. If desired, contributions may be made to Dayton Children's Hospital or Hospice of Dayton. Online condolences may be sent to www.tobiasfuneralhome.com

Printed in U.S.A.   LP110

"Being deeply loved by someone gives you strength, while loving someone deeply gives you courage."
Dalai Lama

Michael Unger in Union Square, San Francisco, where he met Robin Williams.

However, the **LIGHT** dimmed again in 2021 with stage three cancer. With major surgery and further support from my incredible brother and a great friend, whom I trusted greatly at the time, and my 2021 senior class, we managed to defeat it.

Nonetheless, I was diagnosed with another type of cancer in November of 2021 with surgery to follow in late December. I had to undergo six weeks of radiation, five days a week. Again, a few close friends and my exceptional class of 2022 helped me through it. I refused to miss one day of class. They have always been there for me, and me for them.

> "Cancer is a journey, but you have to walk the road alone. You have to own it. There are many places to stop along the way and get nourishment. You just have to able to take
>
> *Emily Hollenberg, Cancer Survivor*

I've learned that urban students are *relentlessly* resilient. They have taught me that *I* can be relentlessly resilient. Each morning, I look

URBAN TEACHER SURVEY

1. I have been an urban educator for _____50_____ years.
2. I teach _GOVERNMENT, SOCIOLOGY, AM. HISTORY_ classes.
3. Three main characteristics of urban teachers are:
   TOTAL CO   TO STUDENTS
   AUTHENTIC + VULNERABLE
   MAINTAIN HIGH EXPECTATIONS
4. Urban children/teens I serve are:
   INSPIRING, DIVERSE, FUNNY,
5. Three main characteristics of urban children/teens are:
   • PERSISTANT
   • TENACIOUS
   • DEMANDING
6. If I could change/add 2 things about urban schools/education I would
   • LESS TESTING SO CREATIVE TEACHING IS PRIORITY
   • ALL GENRES OF ART AVAILABLE AT HIGH LEVELS
7. Three mentors/colleagues that have influenced/guided me are:
   • DOUG JEFFRIES — EMPATHETIC
   • ERIN DOOLEY —RELENTLESS/FLEXIBLE
   • ALL URBAN TEACHERS WITH COMPASSION & PASSION
8. Five students that have influenced/guided me are:
   • JUSTIN FULLER — OVER OBSTACLES
   • IVORY KENNEDY — CLASS ACT
   • SHELDON BROWN — OVER OB
   • EMMA JOHNSON — CLASS ACT
9. My proudest accomplishment is MY RELATIONSHIP WITH MY WIFE AND OUR DEDICATION TO URBAN PUBLIC EDUCATION

Comments:
• CHILDREN'S VOICES MATTER. URBAN CHILDREN HAVE TO SPEAK LOUDER TO HAVE THEIR VOICES HEARD
• URBAN TEACHERS NEED TO BE HEARD AND UNDERSTOOD. MAKE YOUR VOICE ONE OF THEM!

into the mirror, and I know how lucky I am to face 150 demanding and talented young people. I have inexcusably high expectations for all of them, and they reciprocate the same characteristics. I give them as much perfection of the urban teaching profession that I can. I do it not only for them, but for the men that I served with overseas that never made it back.

Today the **LIGHT** is bright. Listen to each other. Learn from each other.

January of 2022 marks the beginning of my 50th year of urban public school teaching. There have been so many uplifting memories in and out of school. Always, in the journey, there has been a constant: the beautiful students.

It has been an honor and a privilege to TEACH.

We have to strive to keep great urban teachers. The teacher dropout rate is horrific. Within twenty-two months, 25% of teachers leave the profession and in five years 50% leave. They leave for higher pay in another profession or within educational administration. Some leave for military service. Others leave to start a family. Teachers leave because they are unhappy with the conditions in the schools. Some teachers just want out of urban schools and want to transfer to a suburban or rural district.

At risk, marginalized and impoverished students need stability. They need to know that their teacher is returning the next day, week, month and year. We can accomplish this in different ways. We have to boost the status of the profession. It shouldn't be a step to another job. It should be the career that you want to embrace. We have to allow for positive collaboration with professionals within your department, school and district. Prospective college students who want to pursue urban education must be paired with successful and experienced teachers and that should be ongoing. Unions must do more to engage new teachers so that they see the value of their profession. All new teachers should be mentored by another great teacher in the building. New teachers should periodically attend workshops where they can share both positive and negative experiences.

To be a successful and dedicated urban educator, you have to understand justice. You can't grasp the concept of justice until you can see the whole child. We must be brothers, sisters, parents, neighbors and friends. We have to be within their proximity to help them sift through their life experiences. It has been a fifty-year journey, and I've met extraordinary people who advocate for children at risk. We have to find the bravery and courage to embrace hundreds of years of bigotry, racism and separatism that have identified our children. The challenge is to recognize and overcome the brokenness in our urban neighborhoods.

Climbing Higher Mountains

"I'm climbing
I'm climbing
Higher mountains
Higher mountains
Trying to get home
My road been a little rocky on my way home
Trying to get home."

—*Aretha Franklin*

This book is an **INVITATION** to a great and rewarding profession. ●

Image of Michael Unger that went viral on Breast Cancer Awareness Day.

218

"The ability for a group of people to do remarkable things hinges on how well those people can pull together as a team."

Simon Sinek

Acknowledgements

I am not a writer, but I am a storyteller. I had an enormous amount of help coordinating and compiling the stories of incredible people. I offer a special thanks to Lonnie Fleming, Lucas Rhynard, Penelope Fisher, Caleb Earick, Leigha Strozier, Linda Sue Hammond and Tse'Kai Walker for helping me put pen to paper. They have dedicated long hours and their creative writing talents to make me look great.

Mostly, I want to celebrate the students, the talented educators and mentors who shared their reflections. There have been many people who have helped me in my journey. I have the responsibility of making the road for others to follow. All of us must have the will and passion to make our urban educational institutions a place where all of our children can aspire to their highest dreams.

Editor's Note

 Since my early childhood, I have been fascinated by written words and the meanings that they convey. When I was just three, I copied the letters SMYTH'S LIQUOR STORE from a sign I could see from my bedroom window, and I wanted my parents, a minister and a teacher to tell me what it said. After this experience, they decided it was time for me to read and write—then came my deep fascination with books. I began with *Aesop's Fables*, moved to poetry then the usual fairy tales. By eight, I was into biographies and dinosaurs.

After years of a variety of professions, from sales, to counseling, to teaching and owning my own antique business, I find the best part of my day is when I can conclude it by holding a real book in my hands and letting my current mood or latest curiosity govern my reading habits. I enjoy a variety of genres, from war crimes and high mystery, to personal stories. It is fascinating to read about the depths that a human can descend to achieve fame, power or money...perhaps all three...or how high a person can fly because of their passion, their drive and their kindness. Through books, we can momentarily escape into notoriety and crime, or compassion and enlightenment.

It has been a great pleasure for me to edit Michael Unger's first book. He is an inspired and compassionate urban teacher who has spent 50 years of his life working with our children. He tells the stories in his book through the eyes of other great professional teachers but mostly through the lives and words of his students whom he has taught, loved and inspired.

It's been a pleasure, Michael.

Carol Gessner-Livingston, Ph.D.

drgess05@yahoo.com
937-477-0503

CPSIA information can be obtained
at www.ICGtesting.com
Printed in the USA
LVHW051336060323
740968LV00005B/16